What Foster Care Staff Need to Know

Teens in the System Write About What Works

By Youth Communication

Edited by Al Desetta

YOUTH COMMUNICATION

True Stories by Teens

What Foster Care Staff Need to Know

EXECUTIVE EDITORS
Keith Hefner and Laura Longhine

CONTRIBUTING EDITORS
Rachel Blustain, Kendra Hurley, Nora McCarthy,
Giselle Benatar, Jennifer Chauhan, Sheila Feeney

LAYOUT & DESIGN
Efrain Reyes, Jr. and Jeff Faerber

COVER ART
Photo: YC Art Dept.

ISBN 978-1-933939-90-2

Second, Expanded Edition
The first edition of this book was entitled *Let's Talk*.

Printed in the United States of America

Youth Communication ®
New York, New York
www.youthcomm.org

Catalog Item #CW-04

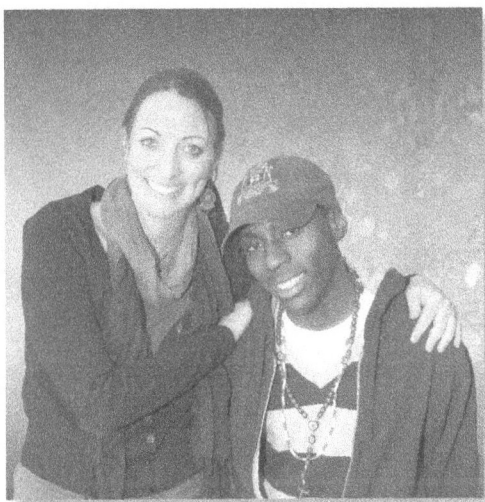

Table of Contents

Contents

Givin' Props to All Staff and Social Workers

Jessica describes how supportive staff have helped her.

Finding a Father in the System

A supportive male staff member breaks down Clarissa's
fears about men.

It May Be Living, But It Ain't Independent!

Staff in the author's group home are not preparing
teens to be independent.

Here Today, Gone Tomorrow

Charlene is devastated when her wonderful social
worker leaves for another agency.

Social Workers: The Good, the Bad, the Overworked

Shanikqua looks at good and bad social work practice.

Listen Up—Let's Talk

Giselle describes four staff types, including the ideal.

Contents

Contents

One Tough Mama

An interview with a group home worker, who talks
about her "tough love" approach.

A Three-Point Shooter

None of Max's group home counselors notice his
depression.

Me and My Mentor

An adult mentor helps Tara learn to trust again.

A New Beginning

When a supervisor inquires about his past, Mohamed
discovers the healing power of connecting with others.

FICTION SPECIAL: Lost and Found

Using the Book

Introduction
for Adults:

Foster youth expect a lot from staff, including emotional support. Yet communication between teens and staff can be hindered by mistrust and even hostility. *What Foster Care Staff Need to Know* is a powerful tool for training staff and helping both teens and staff to communicate more openly and effectively with each other.

In these stories, teens reflect on group home staff, caseworkers, and social workers who have helped them (and some who haven't). You can use the positive and negative experiences described here as case studies to examine good practice, understand where teens are coming from, and show staff how much their actions matter.

The writers in this book offer insightful, provocative accounts of how they have been ignored or misunderstood, as well as validated and saved by sensitive interactions. What comes through most is how a little extra care and attention can make all the difference.

In the first story, Marcus Fowler opens up when a group home staff member shows genuine interest in his painful past. Her extra attention helps him start to get his life back on track. In "Taming My Anger," staff members at a group home for gay and lesbian teens help Tray feel accepted, and show him some more constructive ways to deal with his emotions.

By contrast, several teens write about times that staff could have truly helped them, if only they were paying more attention. A few of Max Moran's group home counselors show interest in him, but none notice that he's going through a deep depression. In "A Good Girl's Turmoil," the author tries to be the perfect group home girl to win the staff's attention and affection, but underneath she feels depressed and lonely. She wishes staff would do more to help the "good residents" with their problems.

These stories also reveal why so many teens in care may

initially be hostile or mistrustful of new staff members. Some recount bad experiences with unprofessional staff. The author of "It May Be Living, But It Ain't Independent," for instance, receives little help in preparing for life after foster care. Instead, her group home staff let their boyfriends sleep over, go out to clubs, and display nasty attitudes toward the residents

For other writers, the problem is bonding to staff who are wonderful—but then leave. When Anne Ueland first goes into foster care she's worried about being treated badly, meets a welcoming and supportive staff member named Kete, and is devastated when they lose contact. And during her 16 months in foster care, Giselle John has become very close to two caseworkers and an educational coordinator in her agency—only to have them disappear from her life when they move on to other jobs.

Still, for many of the writers, the actions of a particular staff member make a lasting and positive difference.

In "Finding a Father in the System," Clarissa Venable describes the challenge of dealing with male staff members after being abused by men in her family. At first she hates Mr. Dugue, a group home staff member, simply because he's a man. But Mr. Dugue breaks down Clarissa's fears with his warmth and sincerity and becomes a father figure.

And in the book's final story, Mohamed Khan keeps a wall between himself and those in his group home who try to get close. But when a supervisor inquires about his past, Mohamed gradually opens up about the abuse he suffered and discovers the healing power of connecting with others.

What Foster Care Staff Need to Know isn't just a tool for staff. It can also help teens to better understand what staff can and cannot do for them. These stories show how both youth and adults can improve communication, and provide insight into the kind of approaches and styles that can lead to strong and satisfying bonds with young people in foster care.

Stephanie Wilson

Opportunity Knocks

By Marcus Fowler

Before I was placed at my group home, I was not motivated to go to school or take my life seriously. I had too much pain in my past to believe the future would be any better.

At my group home it seemed like the other residents weren't doing anything positive with their lives either, so my daily routine became smoking marijuana and going to the park to play basketball. For almost nine months I was not enrolled in school and did not have a job.

During that time, many staff came to talk to me, to set up individual and group counseling. We also had different speakers come to the facility. I only went so my allowance wouldn't be taken away. I never did take the meetings seriously.

One day I was in my room smoking a cigarette when Ms. Gaskin, one of the staff members, came into my room and asked if she could talk to me. I said, "Get the hell out of my room" and continued to smoke. But Ms. Gaskin didn't leave. She was persistent.

"Marcus, it's very important that I talk to you now," she said.

Feeling frustrated, I told her to talk. She said she knew that I didn't have a pleasant childhood. She said she knew I was abandoned by my parents, abused by my grandmother, placed in the system at 12 years old, and that I had run away from those group homes. Then she said she was concerned about me.

What Ms. Gaskin said struck a chord in me, because I could tell that she was serious. For the first time in my life, I felt that someone cared about me, wanted to know about me, and wanted to help. Other staff didn't talk to me. When some did, they didn't seem fully interested so I didn't trust them.

Ms. Gaskin pulled up a chair next to my bed and said, "Marcus, what's going on? You're not in school. You're smoking marijuana too much. And you need to start taking your life seriously."

What Ms. Gaskin said struck a chord in me, because I could tell she was serious.

She was telling me things that I already knew but had refused to deal with. I wanted to cry, but I didn't want to appear soft.

As we talked, I started to get even more scared because I realized that I had nothing going on as far as school or a job was concerned. I felt like it was too late to do anything, but when I told Ms. Gaskin this, she assured me that it's never too late.

It was hard to change my life as a result of one conversation, but as the days passed Ms. Gaskin talked to me often. It felt good. I told her about missing my siblings, thinking of them constantly, and wanting to see them. Ms. Gaskin helped arrange that.

She also helped me enroll in a school program. It was hard at first because my reading and spelling were bad and I didn't feel focused. However, I knew that I had to do something with my life. I couldn't just sit back, reflect on the past, and be mad all the time. I enrolled in a GED prep class and have been studying really hard. I'm looking forward to taking my GED.

Knowing Ms. Gaskin is the best thing that has happened to me in foster care. Nowadays I see so many young Marcuses in the group home, running around, getting high, and basically chilling. If more staff would honestly approach them, I believe they would allow the staff to help.

> *I knew I had to do something with my life. I couldn't just sit back, reflect on the past, and be mad all the time.*

But if the staff comes in with the "I'm just doing my job" attitude, I don't think the residents will feel comfortable sharing their feelings or allowing the staff to help. From the start I trusted Ms. Gaskin, because she was genuinely concerned about what was happening in my life.

Rosa Perin

A Good Girl's Turmoil

By Ijeoma Okolo

During my first few years in the foster care system, I didn't have love from too many people, and I wanted staff's love. So when staff asked anything of me, I did as I was told. I didn't sleep with guys. I didn't do drugs. I began saving money to prepare myself to leave the system. I got accepted into college. I worked two jobs while going to school.

Staff held me up as model resident to other kids, and to new staff, too. Their words gave me confidence. The staff's approval was like the salt that added taste to my life. Since I lived at a residential treatment center (RTC), I didn't have too much contact with the outside world. Staff members were the most important people in my life. Whenever they were disappointed in me, I felt like I was drowning.

Because staff's approval was so important to me, I felt a lot of pressure never to wind up in the "bad girl" category—the ones who did drugs or got pregnant. Sometimes when a resident slept around, the workers would call her a slut. They'd say, "She has no respect for herself. If she were my daughter I would kick her out. She's nasty." They would tell the rest of us not to be like her.

If a resident used drugs, they would call her a crackhead. They'd say, "She's going to end up in jail. She's going to end up homeless. She's going nowhere in life."

Back then I used to go along with staff's comments. Mainly, I didn't want them to say those things about me.

But what everyone saw of me was not who I was. They only saw the surface—how I presented my achievements and my smile. But there was another side of me that I kept secret, that I hid from everyone in the system. That part of me was very angry, very depressed, and very lonely.

I was angry because of the sexual, emotional, and physical abuse I suffered. I was angry because of the rape, and the drug and alcohol abuse from my childhood.

I was also angry because, when I came to the RTC, I never received any real treatment for all the things I went through. I never felt comfortable enough to open up and talk about what brought me into the system. I felt like staff only looked at how I was behaving. If I was being good, then they would label me a good girl. But I never felt like I was really heard, and anger continued to secretly fill me.

I left the residential treatment center when I was 18. I took all the pain that I had buried in me for so long and secretly began to act it out.

In the group home that I moved into I was afraid to lose my reputation as the good girl, so I continued to hide my true feelings. But life in the group home did give me more independence to do as I pleased and go where I wanted to go. I went and discovered my real freedom outside the group home.

In the real world, I was a stranger, unknown. No one had any expectations of what I should be and no one categorized me. Out in the real world I felt my heart surge like a bird taking flight, a bird rising from its anguish and celebrating the freedom of being its true self. Had anyone known how I was acting, I would have ruined my reputation.

I used to drink before I went into care and it was a beautiful feeling. It made me laugh and feel like everything was OK. But I stopped drinking when I went into the system because I was trying to be the perfect girl.

When I moved to my group home, I started drinking again. At first I drank to put myself to sleep, because it helped me get rid of my pain. Usually two were enough to put me to sleep. But eventually I began to drink more and more, whenever I got the chance. I would go out drinking with my new friends. When I was drinking and socializing, I felt happy.

They only saw the surface—how I presented my achievements and my smile. But there was another side of me that I kept secret.

When I went to live in the group home I also began sleeping with men. Because I so badly wanted to embrace the feeling of love, I found myself using sex to hold onto men. I grew up in a home where love was shown through sex. The men in my family began molesting me when I was 5 years old, so it was natural for me to think I could find love through sex.

There were quite a lot of men and boys who I slept with while I was living in the group home. In most cases, I knew them for less than a couple of days before I slept with them. Having men want me made me feel beautiful and erased my sadness. I always felt better when they were holding me.

In my heart I really didn't want to sleep with them, but I thought if I didn't sleep with them I would lose them. I was too scared of being lonely and rejected to say "no." It was as if my heart was running a race for love and I didn't want to lose.

But most of these men didn't stick around too long. When

some left, I just said that it was their loss. But with others, it felt like I was gone.

So doing these things didn't make me happy in the long run, but in the short run they did. Often the happiness I felt from drinking or from being with men was the only happiness I had. So it made me angry to think that if staff knew what I was doing, they might judge me badly. I didn't think I should have to feel ashamed. Besides, I did those things in order to break free. Being the perfect girl was hurting me too much.

Last year, when I moved into my own apartment, my loneliness hit me harder than ever. At first I was drinking a lot with a close friend, who I was also sleeping with so I wouldn't feel so alone. But being on my own was such a shock that I started to realize that I had to deal with my problems, not escape them with drink and sex. I decided that I needed to be more in control.

Too often, the people who work in the system don't see what's going on underneath. They should know that there's always struggle and pain they do not see.

I was so desperate for a job that I ended up making a promise to God that I would stop drinking if He helped me find one. I kept the promise for a while, but after two good months and no job I went back to drinking. Still, I drank less than I had before, only about once or twice a week.

Then I started writing about my problems. My first story was about feeling ugly and wanting to have love from men. Through writing and rereading my writing, I saw a girl who was in pain, a girl who was losing her identity, a girl who needed help. It made me realize that sleeping with all these men hurt me. I realized that these guys were manipulating me, using me, and it made me feel so much anger that I couldn't go on with it. I had to stop. I made a decision to not sleep with men I really didn't know, and for now I've stopped.

I know that drinking and sleeping with lots of men are not ultimate solutions but only temporary pleasures. Rather than helping my life move forward, they just make it spin in circles. I know that if I continue these things I'll just become addicted to them.

But that doesn't mean that I don't have the desire to do them even now. I still have all those feelings in me that I was never given the chance to explore. Because I never dealt with the pain that brought me into the system, I have to deal with it now that I'm on my own.

People who work in the system want to see us succeed. So when they see us doing "bad" they feel sad or get angry. And when they see us doing well, that's all they want to see. But, too often, the people who work in the system don't see what's going on underneath. They should know that there's always struggle and pain they do not see. They shouldn't try to make us conform to how they think we should behave. They should help us express our pain and release it.

Ijeoma was 21 when she wrote this story. She has since graduated from college with a business degree.

Eric Green

She Tells Me That She Loves Me

By Cecilia Maneiro

Three months before my 15th birthday, I started to change. I started hanging out with my friends and smoking and drinking. I was out late all the time. If my mom had sat me down and asked, "Why are you changing?" I would have told her that I was feeling sad and depressed.

I felt that way because my sister had run away not long before and that changed my life. My sister and I were always close. We talked about what type of boys she liked or how her day was. But I didn't know that she was going to run away. I though it was messed up how she left me at home by myself.

After she left, I didn't have anyone to talk to. I hated being the oldest in the house. I had so many things to do, like cleaning and taking care of my little brother. It felt like too much responsibility for me at age 14.

I also felt like my mother wasn't thinking about the love I needed from her after my sister was gone, or how it felt to me to be responsible for my little brother. I felt like she was only thinking about my little brother and herself.

When I tried to talk to my mother about how I was feeling, it felt like she was pretending to listen but she didn't seem to hear what I said. She didn't say "I love you" or give me a hug. When I started to act out, I didn't expect her to stop talking to me or cut me off, but that's what happened. I started to feel like no one loved me, like I didn't exist any longer.

I wanted to go outside with my friends because they made me feel loved. And smoking and drinking helped me escape from some of my problems.

But soon my grandmother called the child welfare agency and told them that I was outside, hanging out and smoking weed. Although I realized later that going into foster care was for the best, when I first went into the system I was upset. I felt like my family disowned me. I was feeling upset and depressed about myself, and I felt angry because I couldn't be with my friends all the time.

When I tried to talk to my mother, it felt like she was pretending to listen. She didn't say "I love you" or give me a hug.

For a while after I went into care, I didn't talk to anybody about my feelings. I just had the same thoughts running through my mind: "Nobody wanted to love me or listen to me." At that time I just had hate for everybody. I was messing up in school every day and getting kicked out. The staff tried to talk to me and treated me nicely but I just wouldn't talk to them about anything.

Then I met a staff member named Marilyn Perkins and she became like a second mother to me. She understood what I was going through. She showed me love, she listened, and she was really there for me.

Ms. Perkins is short, about 5'2," and has light skin. She is a calm, laid-back person. She is always happy. She talks to me in a respectful way. She gives me good advice. I tell her about everything because I really trust her.

The first thing I told her I needed help with was school, and she helped me by listening to me and giving advice. She motivated me to do better in school by helping me with my homework (because I never did it). Before I knew it I was passing my classes.

I feel like someone loves me now, somebody who can sit down and talk to me like any normal parent would.

She also told me to try to stop thinking about the past and to move on. She told me that the things I've gone through would make me stronger in the end. Her words made me feel calm.

Then we started to get closer, because one day she and I had a really good talk together. She asked me what I was going through. I got to express how I felt when I was living at home with my mother and how I got put in the system.

My story came out in a rush. "Well, when I wasn't in the system I was out on the streets and I didn't care no more," I told her. "I got into the system because of my grandmother. I wasn't listening to anybody. I thought that no one loved me, so I started hanging outside and not going to school."

"I know what you are going through and I can relate," she said. Then she told me, "I could see that you needed someone to love you." I felt so close to her at that moment.

After that, I began to talk to her more often. I don't always get a chance to, because she has a lot of work to do when she's here. But sometimes she brings her daughter on the weekends and I talk to her, too. That makes me feel like part of her family.

I feel like someone loves me now, somebody who can sit down and talk to me like any normal parent would. I trust Ms. Perkins, because she doesn't tell anybody the things I have told her about my past.

My life has been different in so many ways ever since I met her. I don't feel so angry and alone anymore. That helps me calm down. Now I go to school and don't cut.

I still feel upset a lot because my family and I have not worked things out. That's why Mrs. Perkins asks me, "What's wrong with you?" all the time when I see her. She also tells me that she loves me. That helps me move on and do what I have to do for myself.

Cecilia was 17 when she wrote this story.

Gabriel Appleton

Nice While It Lasts

By Anne Ueland

When they took me away from my parents I was relieved, because I wouldn't have to be abused anymore. My caseworker took me to the hospital to be tested for abuse. I was crying the whole time I was in the waiting room. I was so scared.

Two days later, the nurse told me that they'd found a placement for me. I didn't want to move there because I didn't think anyone would care about me, but I turned out to be wrong. In the years to come I would meet many caring people in my placements. The only thing was, it sometimes seemed that as soon as I got close to someone, it would be time for that person to move on.

That night my caseworker brought me to a diagnostic center, which is a place where you live temporarily while your social worker decides the best placement for you. At the center, when I got upstairs, I saw a bunch of girls sitting in the living room. The staff told me that I was going to be the baby of the house, because I was only 12. All of the girls came up to talk to me. They could see I was sad and were making jokes to make me laugh. Earlier, one of the residents had told me that they were going to treat me bad, so I couldn't believe how nice and friendly they were being. Goes to show you, don't always listen to what everyone tells you. You need to find out on your own.

The staff person on duty that night seemed very welcoming. But when they told me the rules I got upset. They were too strict. I could make only three phone calls to my mother each week and could only talk for 15 minutes. I could make only one friendship call each week for the same amount of time. The staff person told me that I had to attend school in the building and that residents were not allowed outside without staff. I felt like I was in jail.

I could make only three phone calls to my mother each week. I felt like I was in jail.

For the first month I was going in and out of depression. I was so upset about my life. I felt like everything was going downhill for me. My mother would call me every day telling me how much she wanted me home, but I had so many mixed feelings about going home. I wanted to go home because I could tell she missed me, but I didn't want to go because I knew the abuse would continue.

Plus, even though most of the people at the center were nice, I still felt very alone. I felt that no one loved me and that no one knew what I was going through. After being in placement for three months, I started to fall into a very deep depression. I started to get a lot of flashbacks to the abuse that went on while I was living with my mother and father. I couldn't believe that I'd been put through so much pain. I decided to stop eating, maybe because eating was the only thing I had any control over at that time.

Eventually my social worker and all the staff members decided it was necessary to put me in a hospital. I only stayed in the hospital for a week. I ate in there so I could get out.

When I came back from the hospital I saw a staff member I had never seen before. She was tall and had brown skin. Her name was Kete James. Kete had worked there before but left to have a baby. She seemed so nice.

Kete was different from some of the other staff I met. She didn't seem as if she was in the job for the money. She seemed to really care about all of the residents. While she was there we grew really close. We used to always hang out together on trips out of the house. I could tell her anything I was feeling and she wouldn't get upset with me. And I could trust that she wouldn't tell any of the residents. I knew that if I talked to some of the other staff, they would tell my business to everyone.

When Kete was on duty I felt less down. She made sure I ate. She also believed that I could make it in life if I put my mind to it. She made me feel loved, cared for, and no longer alone. I felt as if Kete were the mother I never had.

After nearly a year in the center, I heard the bad news. It was time for me to go to another placement. I used to want to leave the diagnostic center, but when the day finally came I wanted to stay. I had gotten attached to everything, including Kete.

I was lucky Kete was on duty the night I was leaving because I needed someone to comfort me. It was so hard saying goodbye to her. I felt like I would never see her again. Kete made such a big difference in my life and I will never forget all she did for me. She treated me like her daughter. She made me a stronger person.

In my next home the girls were nice to me but I remember going to bed crying. I missed Kete very much. I didn't think I would ever meet anyone like her again. I didn't think anyone could have a heart like hers. Most people I'd known before placement had no hearts. I had expected the same in placement. But I'd met Kete, and it wasn't long before I met many other people who cared.

Unfortunately, I've lost contact with many of them, too. There was my social worker, Angela, who would take time out of her day to check up on me at school. She would also call from her house to see if we were doing fine. Angela helped me open up more about my feelings.

I also got close to my roommate Renarta. Every time I looked like I was down, she'd come over to talk with me.

When Kete was on duty I felt less down. She made sure I ate. She also believed that I could make it in life.

Ericka, a staff member, helped me build a closer relationship with God. Every night she was on duty we would pray together. After a while Ericka started inviting me to church, and almost every Sunday she would do my hair in a different style. I felt that everything I was praying for was coming true. My schoolwork was improving and so were my relationships with the people I loved. I felt better than ever before.

But one day in July, my roommate Renarta told me she was moving back to her mother's house. I was upset, but felt a little better when I realized how close her mother lived to our group home. Then, about nine months later, Ericka left too. I felt bad that she left, but people have to move on with their lives. Still, it's hard to get close to people only to have them move on.

Around the same time that Ericka was leaving, I was going to be discharged to live with my mother. I wasn't that happy about going back to my mother because I knew that she hadn't changed. I also knew I had found friendship and love in my placements. I went home, but after two days I came back. To this day I am still in placement and am very close to a staff member named Theandre.

Although it's hard to have people come into my life and then move out again, I want to continue staying in placement because it's been good for me. The people I met have made me the person I am today. I am one strong individual. Sometimes I still get depressed, but when I do I think about all the people who have helped me and remember the advice they gave me: "Be who you are," "Don't let the past bother you," and "Keep your head up." It makes me feel better.

Anne was in high school when she wrote this story.

Shaun Bryan

The Staff at My Group Home Make a Difference

By Sandra Negron

Before I entered the lovely doors of my group home, I'd been in two other group homes in two other agencies where I hadn't been happy. I didn't like the agencies or homes because I felt like nobody cared about me. I was allowed to do anything I wanted and the staff gave me a lot of freedom because they knew that I wasn't staying there for long. At the time, I didn't care because I was running the streets.

The house they placed me in next was worse. When I looked inside the refrigerator, I was shocked by what I saw. There wasn't anything there. I said to myself, "Here goes another house with staff that doesn't care."

I was right. If we went AWOL, we'd be put on restriction for just two to three days. And the staff would make fun of residents because of the way they looked or acted. Once a resident came in the house who looked like she didn't have a lot of clothes, and when the girls started making fun of her the staff joined in. I really couldn't do anything but feel bad for her. I said to myself, "I have to get out of this house because it's just like mine. I guess all group homes are the same—they just don't care."

I went back home for a couple of months but that didn't work out, so I went back in the system. Not knowing where I was going, I got out of the agency's van and stepped inside the new house. All the girls were sitting around laughing and playing Monopoly. There were about eight of them, and another three were in the living room talking on the phone and watching television.

I was surprised by it. Everybody was getting along so well. I couldn't believe what I was seeing—a house full of respectful people.

I was the type to be so disrespectful to people—not listening to my elders, yelling at people, and being rude—but when I went inside that house my whole attitude changed. I wasn't yelling at people or being rude because it wasn't in the environment there. Why? The staff were so respectful. The way they talked to the girls made it seem like they were involved in their lives and wanted to see them make something out of themselves when they left the system.

When I first got there, there was a girl who had been in that house for about three years. She was leaving the group home and going to an independent house in the same agency. When she told the staff that she was going to the other place, they were cheering her on and were giving her hugs. At that moment I said to myself, "That was so nice. The staff must have really been there for her to make it so far." I also thought about how that girl was not disrespectful and going on to better things because of her attitude, so I decided to start being nice, too.

That was a while ago. Now I'm the oldest resident here. I've been here for two and a half years and I've seen people come and go. When they go, they still call the staff to talk and the staff is so happy to hear that they're safe. The staff also makes sure that the girls are still doing what they have to do, such as going to school, maintaining a job, and having a roof over their heads.

I know that all group homes are not the same. This new one taught me that some staff members actually do care. So, since my group home has such good staff, I wanted to ask them what their secret is so that maybe staff members at other group homes could learn something from it.

A staff member named Ms. B said she makes "an effort to be understanding of the residents' situations and problems." She understands that we're in group homes because we've been neglected or abused. She is willing to talk to us at anytime.

Ms. B is about 5'4", has dark brown hair and is always smiling. When I was interviewing her she was very open and that's what I like most about her. When I asked her questions she never backed down and you could tell that she really wanted to work with the kids.

Everybody was getting along so well. I couldn't believe what I was seeing—a house full of respectful people.

Ms. B says she has kids of her own, but wants the best for the kids that she works with as well. She hopes to make a positive impact on their lives. She wants to be more than their friend. She wants to be their mentor.

She told me, "It's stressful living with a house full of strangers. It affects the kids because some of them want to be home with their families and they can't go back, so it leaves them with a lot of anger and different mixed feelings. It makes the kids want to leave."

I agree. I think that it is stressful living with a bunch of strangers because everyone has her own personality and different way of looking at things, and that can be hard. But staff people like Ms. B make it easier by talking to us and making it fun so we won't leave and get into trouble.

I talked with another staff member named Mrs. D, who I've known since I've been there. She's been working in my house for about four years. She has light brown hair and is always joking around, but she takes her job seriously. She says she likes "working with the kids because the kids look up to the staff members like role models," and that's what she tries to be for them so that they can make it in life.

Mrs. D gets really close to the girls in the house. She's like a real friend to them because she feels that the girls need an older support in their lives since they are not living with their families.

Mrs. D has known a certain girl for about three years who I also know very well. We used to always hang out and have a lot of fun. This girl went to a new group home because she was always AWOL and getting high. When this girl calls, Mrs. D makes sure she's doing well and isn't getting into trouble. She's a staff member who doesn't give up.

I think that it's good to get close to the residents because they need all the support. When they don't get that support, it might make them go down the wrong path, because every child needs somebody to guide her in the right direction. When the kids don't get it, they tend to fall.

Good staff members are critical to running a good group home. In my agency, staff members care for the residents and I think that's why I've seen many foster kids from my agency go to college and make it. One girl I was very close to left my agency and is now in the Air Force in Texas. Another girl I used to live with left to go to college. So miracles can happen in foster care. If the staff members are role models, the kids will follow.

Sandra was 15 when she wrote this story.

Dani Reyes Mozeson

Do the Staff Really Care?

By Anonymous

To all staff members—don't take what I have to say personally. I've been in the system for two years and what I have to say needs to be heard.

Most of the dozen staff I've had in the two group homes where I've lived don't seem to care about the well-being of the kids, but only about the paychecks they get every two weeks. Their attitudes make me want to throw up.

Not all staff members are like this. Many staff members know how to relate to the residents. They can get along with them without having problems. Some of the staff in the group home where now I live were in foster care and came back into the system to work as childcare workers.

They are the ones who show patience and understanding towards what the residents are experiencing, and who are able to sit down with the residents and listen to their problems. For example, Lloyd, a staff in my group home, will always give me a pep talk when he sees that I'm doing the wrong thing in the house.

But many others don't have that experience and understanding. When you take a job working with kids in the system, it's going to be difficult dealing with the attitudes and different mood swings of the residents. But many staff don't have a lot of patience dealing with the emotions of the kids. Instead of being understanding, they come to work with their own attitudes and problems and take it out on the residents.

For example, there was a girl named Shawna who came to my group home upset because it was her first placement. When Ms. D, the staff, asked Shawna to do her chore, she refused. Ms. D angrily told Shawna that if she was going to be a resident there, she was going to have to help clean the house or else she could pack her bags and leave. Shawna started cursing at Ms. D. Shawna finally settled down after several residents helped to calm her. Ms. D should have handled the situation by talking to Shawna in a pleasant voice instead of an angry voice.

Ms. D should have handled the situation by talking to Shawna in a pleasant voice instead of an angry voice.

Sometimes the staff doesn't do the jobs they're supposed to do. In my group home, the night staff is responsible for preparing breakfast for the residents. But one morning no one prepared breakfast.

Judy was on duty when I came downstairs. I asked her if she could prepare breakfast. She said, "I'm not preparing any breakfast because they don't pay me enough money to serve breakfast when I come on duty."

Then she said, "I don't care about anybody in this group home, and the only reason why I'm working here is for the money. I couldn't get any other job."

Another incident convinced me that some staff are working just for the money. When I came home one day in the summer from football practice at 2 p.m., so hungry I was ready to fall out, I walked into the staff's office requesting permission to make something to eat. The staff on duty at the time, Michelle, told me it was against the rules. (We're only supposed to eat lunch in the group home between 12 and 12:30.)

"Who the hell do you think you are coming in this house at 2 o'clock asking for lunch? You should have ate before you came home from practice," Michelle said.

I asked her to stop cursing at me but she refused. I began to curse back at her. I knew I was wrong for cursing back at her, but I just wanted her to see how it felt.

The staff should take time to speak to Bob instead of always calling the police.

There is another kid in my group home named Bob. Every time Bob gets mad about something, he curses the staff and starts destroying the house. The staff then gets another resident to beat Bob up to calm him down, but when that doesn't work the staff then call the police. I know it's not easy dealing with violent residents, but the staff should take time to speak to Bob instead of always calling the police. The staff knows Bob has a lot of problems but they don't try to deal with them. The staff should know how to calm an angry resident down. If an individual is destroying the house, staff should restrain that individual until he calms down. Many residents get their attitudes from the staff.

One reason why there are so many problems between staff and residents is because some staff members are always ready for a confrontation. Every time they do something for a resident, they act like they're doing them a favor. Some staff members think that most teenagers in care are a bunch of hoodlums and that's why our parents put us in the system.

The staff should learn how to communicate and relate to the

teens. They have to take the chance to get know each resident. Instead, most staff just read the residents' records when they come into care and hold that against them.

The staff also needs to be more humble and not react to negative things they encounter. I understand they are human beings who have feelings, but they have to be the mature ones and remember they are working with teens who have been abused — sexually, mentally, and physically.

The agencies need to better train their staff in how to deal with residents who have been abused. The staff should learn how to resolve conflicts and how to calm residents down when they became angry.

One way to train the staff is to have foster youth participate in the training by telling their stories and giving the staff suggestions on how to handle kids who were abused, especially when they're coming into care for the first time. The staff needs to be trained in how to recognize behavior problems linked to abuse, and how to let the youth express their feelings both one-on-one and with the whole staff listening.

The agencies need to hire people who care for the well being of the teens. The agencies should require a bachelor's degree in social work and two years of experience in working with teens after college. Something needs to be changed in the way many of the group home staff are hired.

The author was 18 when he wrote this story.
He graduated from college in 2003.

Fernando Garcia

Givin' Props to All Staff and Social Workers

By Jessica DeSince

I hear so many horror stories about social workers and staff that it makes me wonder—what the hell is going on here? I had a social worker who worked wonders for me. If she didn't keep after me to do right, I wouldn't be where I am today. The social worker I currently have is also nice.

Some youth complain that social workers don't answer calls. But when I needed to speak to Ms. F (my old social worker), she was always there. Some group home residents complain that social workers are always in meetings. But it's important that they have meetings to discuss us.

Other residents say social workers and staff don't listen. But in order for them to listen to us, we have got to listen to them. In my experience I've seen that most residents don't listen to what staff say. I agree with the expression, "If you don't listen, why should I?"

I've heard so many complaints that the staff talk about us behind our backs. That they don't respect us or that they curse at us. I have never had a staff member disrespect me or come out of his or her face by cursing at me. I've never had to deal with these problems.

I've been in two group homes. One was a placement for pregnant mothers. The second one, where I'm residing right now, is a long-term group home. Both are great! At my first group home I had my own room and space to do whatever I wanted to do.

We'd go to ILS (independent living skills) meetings that they set up for us. The staff really cared and didn't talk about you behind your back.

*I*n the group home I'm in now, it's real nice. It's three bedrooms in a co-op apartment building. You share a room with another girl and we have our own bathroom. I go to a life works program where we talk about our future, AIDS, hygiene, anything.

When I came into foster care, it was a new world for me. Not being able to do what I wanted was hell. Not being able to eat when I wanted was a drag. I actually had to ask to use the phone! I lived with my

I thought I knew it all and no one could tell me anything. When I met my social worker, Ms. F, she changed that quick fast.

grandmother for 15 years and I got to do whatever I wanted. So adjusting to foster care life was disturbing.

So when I came into care I didn't listen to anyone. I did whatever I wanted. I thought I knew it all and no one could tell me anything. When I met my social worker, Ms. F, she changed that quick fast.

She was the one person who took an interest in me. She overlooked the way I acted. She took my case when she had the opportunity to give it to another social worker. She said the reason she took my case was because I reminded her of when she was younger.

Ms. F made me start carrying myself like a lady. I didn't care about how I looked. She gave me advice about dressing myself properly. She was there when I needed someone to talk to. She showed me how to look out for myself as well as my children. She was the shoulder to cry on when I needed to cry.

I think we underestimate some of the social workers out there. You have to remember that they are given 25 or more clients to work with. You can't expect them to perform miracles. We aren't the only ones on their caseloads. You have to meet them halfway.

Jessica was 17 when she wrote this story.

Jamaal Pascall

Finding a Father in the System

By Clarissa Venable

"Hello, my name is Mr. Dugue. What's yours?"

I looked at him and hated him already. It was my first day in the group home and Mr. Dugue was one of the staff members. I hated him because he was a man. I couldn't stand men after what men did to me in my family.

I thought the only one who loved me in my family was my mother. I was adopted when I was 17 days old. When I was adopted my mother was already 52. She adored me because I was her last adopted child and the baby in the family.

My three adopted brothers were 13 to 27 years older than me. When I was young my mother used to spoil me and her sons didn't see anything wrong with that. To them it was natural to spoil a baby. But as I got older, things started to change.

My brothers had been used to getting all the attention, especially my mother's youngest son, Lenny, because he was my mother's last baby. But after I came, my mother seemed more distant with him and Lenny didn't like that—not one bit.

By the time I was 9 and 10 years old, my brothers were abusing me emotionally and physically. When they came home, they would come straight to my room. I used to be so scared. I'd hear them come in and pretend that I was asleep. Then they would come and shake me and start the abuse.

My mother never knew what was going on. For all she knew we were a happy family. I wanted our family to be perfect, like the families on TV. I used to think that if they could get along, why couldn't we be like that?

I hated him because he was a man. I couldn't stand men after what men did to me in my family.

By now I had already started to fall apart. From all the abuse my brothers gave me, I started changing dramatically. In school I used to be a straight A student. Now I could barely maintain a C.

I used to be outgoing and I was everyone's friend. If you needed someone to talk to, I was always there. Now I didn't give a damn about no one and was always starting fights. I felt I could take all the anger out on the person I was fighting.

I just fell away from my family. I started coming in whenever I wanted and doing whatever I wanted. I didn't care about anyone. Not even myself.

One day when I came home my brother James was high on crack. He started punching me like I was his worst enemy and busted my lip, both of my eyes, and knocked up my ear. (Up until this day, I can't hear well out of that ear.)

That night I put ice on my face and tried my best to get the swelling down. I didn't go to sleep that whole night because I was scared. In the morning, my mother thought I had a fight on the street. I wanted so bad to tell her that it was her son, but I didn't have enough courage.

The next day I went to court. I was in shock when my lawyer just came out and said, "She's being abused." The judge said, "For now, she's going to a group home."

I said bye to my mother. She was crying. I was real scared about going to a group home.

The van came to take me away. I said to myself, "No more men to look at." And for the first time in a long time, I smiled.

I was shaken awake by my caseworker and she told me we were there. I looked up and saw a big house. It was blue and white. I got out of the van and walked to the front door. My caseworker rang the bell and a pleasant looking woman came to the door and said, "Hi, my name is Ms. Jordon." I said "Hi" and went inside.

The place looked nice. It was furnished well for a group home, I thought. I expected it to be like a shelter because of the name, "Sheltering Arms." And even though I had never been to a shelter, I knew they weren't nice.

I was led to the back office and gave them my name, my age, and other information. I was so happy not to be with my family that all I did was smile through everything. I was thinking, "No more men!" I was real happy to be in a house that was all girls.

I was sitting there smiling when I heard a deep voice. I was thinking, "Damn, what kinda lady has a voice like that?" I got ready to greet the lady when all of a sudden a man came in saying, "Hi, my name is Mr. Dugue. What's yours?"

I instantly started crying. I was so hurt. With all my problems with my adopted brothers, how could they put me in a group home with a man?

The first thing I asked was, "Are there any more men?" Ms. Jordon said there were not. I just said to myself, "I'll stay away from him."

The next day was good. The girls in the group home were nice. I had a best friend in there named Carlean. She showed me that there will always be good friends.

Since she was being nice to me, I let go. Like I said before, I didn't care about anyone, but she was so nice to me that I thought, "I guess there's nothing wrong with having a best friend."

Carlean and Mr. Dugue were talking one day when I went in the office. He said hi. I said hi and left. It surprised me that he was nice to me. No man ever said hi to me, really seeming like he meant it.

But during the next couple of days I found out that he was so sweet and so nice that I had to like him.

Whenever he saw me upstairs by myself just thinking about old times, he would come over and talk to me. Whenever he saw that I was sad because I was thinking about my mother, he would come over to me and make me laugh. He would say something out of the blue that you weren't even thinking of.

Mr. Dugue showed me that not all men are the way my brothers were.

Like I would be in my room, or in the living room reading, or watching television, when Mr. Dugue would fly in the room and jump in front of me. Then he would fly back out of the room.

We also would play our special game. Mr. Dugue would swear that I passed gas. Then he would take the Lysol can and spray the room or around me.

Mr. Dugue showed me that not all men are the way my brothers were, even though it took me a while to really trust him.

I started really trusting him one night when we were talking and playing around. When it was time for me to go to bed, I went upstairs and he came upstairs. I told him good night. He said, "Good night, daughter."

That really touched my heart. I never had any male tell me that I was his daughter. I also thought that I would never see the day when one did. So when he said that, I knew that I had the father I never had before.

When I got to know people on the block and started breaking curfew, he taught me that it was OK to have friends but it wasn't OK to break curfew. He told me that if I kept breaking curfew, I was going to get in trouble and eventually get discharged.

One time I had a problem with an old boyfriend who lived around the corner. Mr. Dugue told me not to talk to the guys around there. He explained that the boys around the area were no good. They were all in a gang and it wouldn't be good to get involved with them.

He taught me that school came first before anything. He said that there's no future if there's no school. He told me that if I didn't get an education, I was going to be a bum. After he told me that, I went to school again and had a lot of friends.

He made my self-esteem go back up. I really started caring about myself and others.

The only thing I regret now is not being at Sheltering Arms anymore. I had a problem in the group home, so they moved me. But I still got all the lessons "down pat" that Mr. Dugue taught me.

Clarissa was 20 when she wrote this story.

It May Be Living,
But It Ain't Independent!

By Anonymous

Many people wake up to see breakfast on the table, a freshly cleaned house, or to a friendly "Good morning." Well, not me. I wake up to a nasty house that has a bad odor and garbage everywhere.

The story I'm about to tell you about my Independent Living group home (for teens who are getting ready to age out of the system) is pitifully true. All names have been changed to save the agency involved from embarrassment, and to ensure that the people who placed me in this facility won't try to take a buyout.

Imagine getting ready for school and you see a guy is sitting on the couch like he lives in your group home. Well, he doesn't

(All names have been changed.)

live there—he's the boyfriend of one of the staff members. Now, I know for a fact that staff members are not allowed to have their boyfriends visit the group home, let alone spend the night. Well, come to my placement and you'll see more than you bargained for.

When I first came to Independent Living, I didn't realize I was in for such big treats. I always thought that Independent Living houses were supposed to prepare teens to live on their own. The only thing I'm being prepared for is welfare.

For example, my social worker Mr. Slow (if I may call him that) doesn't speak very good English. Now, tell me, how are you going to ask for a week-end pass, if your social worker thinks you're calling him an $&%^$?

Mr. Slow doesn't know how the girls are doing in school, or even if they are in school. But this is the guy the system hires to look out for our needs.

Mr. Slow doesn't stop by or even call to see how the residents are doing. He doesn't know how the girls are doing in school, or even if they are in school. But this is the guy the system hires to look out for our needs.

My staff members are really bugged out, OK? I'm going to describe all three of them.

First you have Ms. Davis. She's the one who doesn't care where your life is going or if the system is planning to throw you out. Just take her to a club. If you're not going to show us the attention we need, why take the job? If you're not going to help us to be independent, then what are you here for? I know you're not here to take us to a club.

With the time and energy it takes to go to a club, Ms. Davis could let us know the real deal. Sit all of us down and tell us about places to get good bargains on furniture. Tell us how to manage our money. Tell us how to go on apartment hunting interviews. Just don't tell us the world is an easy place and then take us to a club.

Then you have Ms. White. She's cool. She has a sense of her job. She tells us we should buy little things for our apartments. She sometimes takes us to stores to buy dishes and stuff. Only thing I would change about her is her attitude.

One time she had an argument with a girl in my house. Ms. White got mad and called her a stupid $(%*&$ because she failed her GED by one point. Now tell me, was that type of behavior necessary?

Third, you have Ms. Gibbs. She proves that "not all staff are bad." I can honestly say she cares. She tries to help us educationally and in any other way that will help us gain knowledge about Independent Living. She has her little ways, but the things she does to help us make up for that. She gives us tips on where to look for jobs. She does her job to the fullest and we need a lot more staff like her.

Then you have Ms. Gibbs, who proves that not all staff are bad. I can honestly say she cares.

But it's not just the staff who seem to be a little immature. It's the residents also. The girls in my house need to stop talking about people. All they do is gossip, gossip, gossip. And they used to sneak guys in. They have a lot to learn about self-respect. They curse like pirates and have no courtesy for anyone's company.

I know you're wondering how I live through all this without getting stressed. Well, it's not easy, but I manage. I go straight to my room. Since I'm the only one with a single room, I can sort of get away.

I know some of you out there may be going through the same things. But don't give up. If you feel yourself getting upset to the point that you can't take it, then go for a walk or try doing something constructive. I think if you stay in the house that's when the animosity builds up. Do everything you have to do, like your chores or whatever else staff asks of you. That's how I try not to get caught up in the nonsense.

I hope all Independent Living placements aren't like mine. They should have a hotline that teens in group homes can call if they want to ask a question about living on their own.

But in the meantime, remember—don't let your house stress you, and never give up.

The author was 19 when she wrote this story.
She graduated from community college in 2002
and went on to study school counseling.

Yvonne Chen

Here Today, Gone Tomorrow

By Charlene Carter

Mrs. Heyward was a wonderful social worker. Though she always had phone calls to return and paperwork to complete, she never got upset if one of us girls in the group home needed her. She'd make herself available, and not only when we got into trouble. She treated each of us a bit differently, according to our personalities, and even got along with one girl who had a nasty temper and rarely got along with anyone. Mrs. Heyward cared about us and we could tell. She treated us all with respect, so we respected her, too. She was down with us group home girls.

Whenever I had some free time, Mrs. Heyward would let me stay in her office while she worked. Sometimes I spent hours there. I remember how good it felt when she complimented me. "I have heard that you are obeying the house rules and keeping out of trouble," she'd say. "That's very good."

How nice that made me feel, like I was special.

For a long time, I thought all social workers were nice like her and I assumed that she was around to stay. I was wrong.

One day it happened. It was the middle of the afternoon. The mood in the group home felt strange. Usually, a staff member is talking to a resident, the telephone is ringing, or an agency worker is visiting. But that day it was very quiet. So quiet it felt lifeless.

When I walked into the living room, I got the shock of my life.

"Mrs. Heyward is leaving the agency," Mrs. Quan, a staff said.

"Why?" Jessy asked.

"Apparently she found another job at a different agency."

I was sure they did this to torture me. To see if I would break. Mrs. Heyward was one of the few people who I could relate well to and the one who got things done for me. She was dedicated to my case. Now she was leaving. I would be lost without her. I wanted to pack my bags and leave, too, because I was afraid of what would happen next.

But the staff promised me that all of the other social workers who came to the agency would be just as caring and dedicated as Mrs. Heyward. They said I would find others who treated me with as much respect as Mrs. Heyward had. But that hasn't happened, and my life has become so complicated because of it.

Our next social worker was Mrs. W, who came in mid-fall. When it was my turn to meet with her, I didn't feel comfortable around her at all. She had broad shoulders and a big chest and stared at me in a way that made me wonder what she was thinking. She was old and very demanding. She insisted that I answer her questions even when I didn't know what she was talking about. Trying to talk to her, I wanted to cry. Instead, I just sat in a daze. I knew that I would get very little accomplished working with her and this discouraged me.

Instead of things getting better now that we had a social worker again, they got worse. Fights broke out. Mia and Tamika got into it. They started an argument that lasted for at least an hour. Paula started throwing and breaking things while Ella screamed, "traitor, traitor, traitor," over and over again. It was as though she was talking to Mrs. W, who wasn't there at the time. No one knew for sure what happened to cause such misunderstandings among us, or whether it was the social worker's fault that things were in an uproar, but the timing was not in her favor. I thought that day would never end.

Life became even more chaotic. Mrs. W had a complicated way of doing things. In response to problems, she would call the group home and ask for a particular girl—instead of meeting with her—to tell her that she was misbehaving. When she was finished scolding that girl, she would speak to another girl and scold her next. It was assembly line scolding.

Mrs. Heyward, of course, would have talked to us in person. She always found out when one of us had a problem and took some time to sit and talk things through. She didn't scold us—she asked us what was wrong. Mrs. W was a different social worker and had a right to handle things differently, but her way just didn't work.

Mrs. Heyward cared about us and we could tell. She treated us all with respect, so we respected her, too.

For many weeks things were in an uproar in the group home. Finally, after six months, Mrs. W left.

Mrs. T, the next social worker, arrived just in time for the agency's picnic. She drank, ate, laughed, talked, and seemed like she might be better than Mrs. W. But she turned out to be a disappointment as well, and soon fights broke out in the group home and we started over with a new social worker.

At the time, Sarah, another girl in my group home, said, "All social workers are like Mrs. W and Mrs. T. They expect you to do for yourself." Sarah was one of the older girls and had been living in the group home the longest. I didn't believe her when she said it. I thought she was just being mean. But when other social workers arrived at the agency who weren't at all helpful, I began to wonder if what she said was true.

I missed Mrs. Heyward. I wished she would have a change of heart and return to the agency. Then things could return to normal like they had been when everyone got along. With Mrs. Heyward, we'd had constructive group activities instead of the gang banging. But she didn't return.

One day, Ella, another resident, said, "I need my working papers. I'm calling the social worker tomorrow for help."

It had been a while since the social worker visited the group home. Everyone was lacking attention and everyone had unmet needs. Ella needed her working papers and Tammy needed her home pass approved. The new social worker hadn't been on a visit in over six weeks. We figured the social worker was busy helping one of us, but when we tried to figure out which one of our cases she was so stuck on that she was unable to get around to the rest of us, we discovered that none of us was being helped.

She didn't scold us—she asked us what was wrong.

I felt that we needed to report her to someone, but we got discouraged after having reported so many other workers without having things improve. We felt that it was a waste of time and effort. We didn't want to start all over when we felt we knew what the outcome would be.

Since then, we have just kept having new social workers come and go. Some were not so good and some were even terrible. The good ones were the rarest and the others were so mean. They were mean, mean, mean. They would miss important appointments and would get us mixed up with each other.

Foster care is not an easy place to grow up in, but having social workers who don't care or who don't try to help you makes things so much harder. When we have poor quality social workers, our day-to-day lives become complicated and hectic. We feel uncared for and that makes us act out in our group homes. This shouldn't be happening. Kids in foster care should have special social workers who care, who can work well with our cases, help us with our goals, and obtain effective results for us. We need more caseworkers like Mrs. Heyward. I still miss her.

Charlene was 21 when she wrote this story. She attended Borough of Manhattan Community College.

Shaun Shishido

Social Workers: The Good, The Bad, The Overworked

By Shanikqua Crawford

In all my years in foster care, I've gone through three social workers—Ms. J, Mrs. M and Mr. F. In my opinion, the first two were good social workers and did their jobs well, but this last one…

My first social worker, Ms. J, was a wonderful person. She was a young, caring woman who was concerned about my needs. She came to my house at least once every two weeks, and she called regularly. Most of the time she called just to talk. She would ask how I was doing at home, in school, or if I needed help with anything. I thought of her as family.

She used to take my sister and me out to dinner and sometimes she would come over to our house for dinner. She always said if we had any problems or needed her for anything, then all we had to do was call.

She was such a sweet lady, and it broke my heart when, after four years of being my social worker, she had to leave. I knew I would never have another social worker like her. Boy, was I right!

When Ms. J left, Mrs. M became my new social worker. She wasn't Ms. J, but she was okay. At first I didn't like her. Now I see that it was partly because she wasn't Ms. J. I thought she was way too nosy, though I guess she was only doing her job.

She came to my school like once a week. I'd be sitting in my elementary school class and look out the door. Guess who I'd see? Mrs. M waving and mouthing, "I'm just checking up on you!"

And whenever she came to the house, the first thing she'd say was: "Can I please use your bathroom?" I don't think she even had to go to the bathroom. She said that so she could take a quick look around the house. (You have to pass every other room to get to the bathroom.)

During her third and final year as my social worker I started to like her, but it was too late because as soon as I started liking her, she got pregnant and had to leave (darn!).

When Mrs. M left, that was it. I got stuck with the worst social worker ever, Mr. F. He's been my social worker for years now and, if you ask me, he should have sought another profession—he's not mastering this one.

Besides the fact that I can't understand a word he says, here's the list of problems I have with him:

1. He barely comes around for visits. You should see your social worker at least four times a month at your agency, if not more. I see Mr. F about once every two to three months. What's that about?

2. He doesn't listen. On those rare occasions when I do see him, he asks me the same questions: "What school do you go to? How old are you?" and, get this, "How do you spell your name?"

He's been my social worker for a couple of years now and he doesn't even know how to spell my name! Judging by his inability to listen, he's definitely not someone who I would pour out my feelings to.

3. He's L-A-Z-Y! Sometimes he's supposed to come by the house to pick up papers that he needs and he won't show up. Instead, he'll call my grandmother and ask her to mail them. And get this—he has a car! He could easily drive himself on over and pick them up!

4. He's disrespectful of our time. He'll call and say he's coming over for a visit at a certain time, say 4:00 p.m. We'll be rushing to get home from school to make sure that we're there on time. And guess what? Mr. F will never show up, and won't even call to say he's not coming.

Usually he'll call the next morning and tell us we have to come down to the office. I remember one time he did that and there was about four feet of snow outside. My grandmother had to drag all of us, even my younger brother who has asthma, out of the house in the cold weather to go see him.

I don't know what the problem is with him. Maybe he feels overwhelmed by all the work

Ms. J would ask how I was doing at home, in school, or if I needed help with anything. I thought of her as family.

he has, or maybe he feels that he's doing his job the best way he knows how. So I was curious to find out other foster kids' experiences with their social workers. Did they have good ones, like Ms. J? Or bad ones? What do they like in a social worker?

Through interviews, I found out that I'm not the only one in foster care who believes her social worker is not doing a good job. Milagros, 14, who lives in a foster home, has a social worker almost as bad as mine. Milagros said she sees her social worker only once a month at her foster agency.

Milagros said that she sometimes gets along with her social worker but whenever she tries to explain something to her, her worker will always argue. "She's very busy most of the time and doesn't have time to discuss," said Milagros. "She got a grouchy attitude and she hardly knows how to communicate."

Ivon, 15, who lives in a foster home, has also had some bad experiences with workers. About her current social worker, Ivon said, "This lady is supposed to be sending me money but never sends it, and she doesn't look out for me or make sure that my foster mother is doing what she's supposed to."

Ivon says she only sees her social worker when she goes to her agency for her independent living program.

Ebony, 15, who also lives in a foster home, said that her current social worker is not doing such a good job because she's not trying to help Ebony's mother get her children back. Ebony says her worker is wasting time on finding the things that her mother does wrong instead of what her mother does right.

Although these kids have had bad experiences with social workers, they have also had good experiences. All of them said that at least one of their workers did her job well.

Ebony has gone through two social workers. Although her current social worker isn't doing a good job, her first worker, Ms. V, did. "If we did something wrong," Ebony said, "she'd tell us to do better. Like if our grades were low, she'd tell us to aim higher. She always tried to help my mother get us back, and when she wasn't there on visits, she would call an hour early to let us know not to come."

Milagros, who's going on her fourth social worker, agreed that her first social worker, whose name she forgot, and her second social worker, Rafael, had done a good job. "They were nice," she said, "they explained everything—the new neighborhoods, how it's gonna be when you're in foster care, what stages I'm going through with the foster parents, if there's any problems to call them, and the regulations."

Joselyn, 17, says that her social worker, Yudelca Mateo, was an excellent social worker who taught her and helped her a lot. But Ms. Mateo left her job as a social worker and Joselyn said she'll miss her dearly.

Joselyn said, "She always had time for me and also she knew

how to take her time with me. She had patience. She knew the way that I was, so she knew the things she could tell me. For example, when I had a problem or when I used to get stressed out, she used to give me advice on how to control my anxiety and how to solve my problems."

The teens I spoke with have had both good and bad experiences with social workers, and, therefore, know what it takes to be a good social worker. They would like to give some advice to social workers, so if any of you are reading this book, maybe you can follow some of these tips (if you're not already doing so).

I feel all foster children would agree with Milagros' advice. Milagros said that social workers "should be nice when kids are nice. They should start believing foster children, too. They always be like, 'Oh, that's not what your foster mother said.' Me and my foster mother is two different people! Hello!"

> *Mr. F doesn't listen. On those rare occasions when I see him, he asks me the same questions: "What school do you go to? How old are you?" and, get this, "How do you spell your name?"*

Ebony also has some good advice. She said, "No matter what the parent did, social workers should always try to get the true story and then help the parents get their children back."

Jocelyn's words to her social workers are, "I'll always appreciate the way they helped me recover from my problem, and I wish that they also could help others and keep up with the patience that they have for foster kids."

Social workers are there to help foster kids. That means they should listen to what the kids tell them, have patience with them, and take the time to help them with their problems. When social workers take their time and listen to their clients, their clients will take the time to listen to them.

Shanikqua was 16 when she wrote this story.

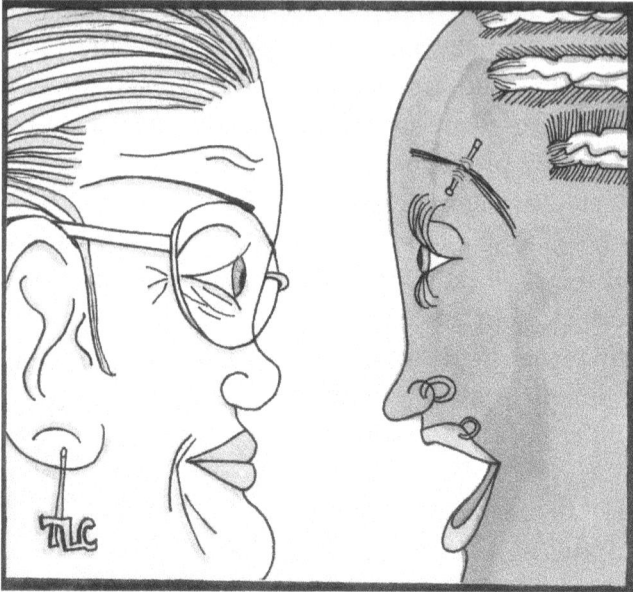

Rosa perin

Listen Up—Let's Talk

By Giselle John

There's a great need for changes to be made in the foster care system, and everyone knows it. One thing I'd like to see changed is how some of the adults working in the system (which includes caseworkers, supervisors, and foster parents) communicate with foster youth. Many adults think that, because they've had certain experiences and training, they know how to communicate with us and are equipped to deal with our problems.

Many adults often don't have the slightest idea of how to handle certain situations, and can complicate things when they try to implement what they think is right. Sometimes they lack knowledge and understanding because they don't take the time to properly evaluate each child's situation.

They fail to listen to the cries of the child who has been pushed to and fro in the system. Many times it's because adults have the impression that "we don't know what we want or what is good for us."

Many adults engage in selective listening, dictatorship communication, and even putting down the young person. This is not appropriate when dealing with a child or young adult.

The Selective Listener: Choosing What She Wants to Hear

Selective listening is when we choose what we want to hear out of a conversation or statement. In many cases, we may hear what was not said. Some adults practice this too often when it comes to dealing with kids in care.

For example, I once spent a long time explaining to my foster mother why my guardian had thrown me out of her apartment before I came into care. It was because I became a Seventh Day Adventist Christian and refused to attend a party that was important to my guardian. My guardian claimed I disrespected and embarrassed her when I did not go. We argued over this, until she said to me, "You got to go. I'll call your mother and tell her. If she don't come and get you by Wednesday, you out of here."

My mother lives in Tobago, in the Caribbean. Because she did not get a flight to New York City as fast as my guardian wanted her to, I had to go into the foster care system for help.

After all this explanation, whenever I spoke about what my guardian did to me, my foster mother would say, "Oh, so that's why you left, huh?" She would say it as if she didn't believe I was thrown out.

I'd always try to tell her that I didn't leave on my own, but I realized that she only wanted to blame me for the problems I had with my guardian. She chose to listen only to what she wanted to hear.

The Boss: Convinced She Is Right

Dictatorship communication, better known as "Boss communication," is when someone takes control of a conversation, and has the impression that what she says is right and needs no competition or correction.

Whenever my foster mother couldn't find something, whether she misplaced it or it was actually stolen, she always thought the thief was a "foster child." You were convicted after one question: "Did you do it?" Even if the reply was "No," she would say, "Well, I think you did it, you are the only one who would be so mean to do something like that. I tell you, I know kids, had nine of my own, raised my own grandchildren, and been a foster mother for years now, so I know when you're lying, because I know kids."

Words can cause as much harm as sticks and stones—even more.

In many cases she was wrong but failed to see it because she always thought she was right, and the fact that she had so many foster kids made her think that she was qualified to judge us. It was either her way or no way, and no one could change her mind.

One time she accused me of stealing her donut and opening her apple juice in the middle of the night. Her own granddaughter confessed, but she did not believe her because she felt that her granddaughter was covering for me. She claimed she raised her granddaughter better than a thief, and if her granddaughter wanted something she knew that she was welcome to ask for it any time. So I was still blamed. In her eyes, members of her family could do no wrong, and foster kids could do no right.

The Put-Down Artist: Full of Harsh Words

"Putting down" means always criticizing someone and not giving them enough credit, even if they deserve it. This is often a problem faced by many children in care. In such cases, a child's self-esteem is lowered and they begin to lack confidence in themselves. Some retaliate by getting into trouble, while others get depressed. All this and more can occur when an adult fails to speak kind, gentle, compassionate, and encouraging words to us.

Let's say a child has worked hard for a grade she earned honestly, a 65 average in a subject that is challenging. Some foster parents, instead of giving words of encouragement such as: "Good, great effort, keep working harder," will dish out insults, for example: "How stupid! Couldn't you do any better?"

The adults need to understand the effect that "putting down" can have on us, especially when they're upset and full of emotion. There's an old saying: "Words spoken in anger can never be recalled." This statement is so true. The hurt that harsh words can cause is unbearable.

A major problem is a lack of balanced communication between adults and children. The adults seem to forget that they themselves are not finished with being educated, and that a child or young adult may know what affects them in a way that the adults may fail to see.

The Listener: Opens the Door to Communication

"Active listening" is one way to improve communication. Active listening is the ability to show the speaker that you heard what was said. This can be done by repeating what the speaker said to you. This proves that you're listening. Asking questions about the subject is another way to prove that you're listening. Also, eye contact and saying little things such as, "Yes, I understand what you're saying," or "Could you repeat what you just said? I didn't quite get that." With active listening on both sides, solutions may be worked out effectively.

If my foster mother had better communication skills, she would have been able to practice active listening. When I explained the reason my guardian kicked me out, she would have been able to clear up any misunderstanding she had, instead of always thinking that I did something wrong.

I think regularly scheduled communication workshops should be put in place for the adults in the system, especially for foster parents, who have to deal with vulnerable children on a daily basis.

In these workshops, effective communication skills should be taught, such as using a good tone of voice, being courteous and respectful, being sensitive to people's needs, and developing the art of good conversation. A good way of giving insights is to have children and young adults give feedback to adults about the effects of positive and negative communication.

Conflict resolution skills should also be taught. It is important to know that while we have different points of view, we should be careful not to state our feelings in an offensive manner but in a respectful way. In my opinion, the old saying, "Sticks and stones may break my bones, but words can never harm me" is not true. I disagree, because words can cause as much harm as sticks and stones—even more.

We all need to develop the ability to listen and engage in more active listening. We should be attentive to what is being said to us. The more we listen, the more we learn, and the better we are at handling obstacles we face or the people we deal with. This goes both ways, for children and adults.

Giselle went on to graduate from college and run
Voices of Youth, a public speaking and advocacy
organization for teens in foster care.

YC Art Dept.

Looking for Common Ground

By Anonymous

In the system there are two kinds of staff members—those you love and those you…well, read on.

I have found my group home supervisor, Mr. W., to be a complete egomaniac who delights in controlling allowances and giving out punishments. Nobody is safe from his power plays, since whomever he can't control, whether staff or resident, doesn't stay at the group home for long. We argue often (every time we meet).

One of our most recent arguments happened at a staff meeting. We were being told about a recreational trip we were taking the following morning. Mr. W. rambled on about how certain people didn't deserve to go on the trip and he pointed me out in front of everyone else as one of those people.

His words set me off, especially since I was not in a particularly good mood. We started arguing and it ended when he said that if I didn't shut up, no one would go on the trip.

If that incident wasn't enough, there was the Fruit Loops Crisis. It began at a house meeting, where Mr. W. said that if we didn't like what was being served in the group home, we should go buy our own food.

Well, I took those words to heart, locked them in my memory, and one day when I had enough money, I decided to act on Mr. W.'s advice.

I went to the store around the corner and bought myself two boxes of 99-cent name brand Fruit Loops cereal (along with other goodies) and proceeded on my merry way back to the group home.

I had my cereal for a while, until the day I came home and found it gone from the cupboard.

A staff member said that Mr. W. had told him to take my cereal and lock it in the office. When I asked Mr. W. about this, he told me that he didn't want us buying our own food. Since this was in contrast to his earlier statements, I decided to argue, which resulted in me being told that I could leave the group home if his rules were not to my liking.

This incident upset me dearly. Not only was my money wasted, but I felt Mr. W. was a two-faced person with a power complex.

I could go into much more detail about how my supervisor has made my life miserable (preventing me from staying after school for extracurricular activities, withholding stipend checks, causing me to be dropped from a school play) but limited space prevents me from doing so.

However, I still have space to speak directly to Mr. W. (if he's reading this book), so here it goes.

You are waiting to tell me about my faults, my ungrateful-ness, and of course, all the things that you have done for me.

For those things that you have done for me I thank you, but

I cannot forgive you for those deeds that have left scars on my soul.

You remember everything you told me about my faults, but you fail to remember the times you tried to make me feel low and ungrateful, when you said things to me that you would never say to your own children.

I hope you remember what I've written here, and perhaps

Nobody is safe from his power plays, since whomever he can't control doesn't stay at the group home for long.

we won't argue the next time we meet, but will instead be able to find some common ground, that won't crumble away when both of us are standing on it at the same time.

The author was 17 when he wrote this story. He later graduated from SUNY-Purchase with a degree in English Literature

YC Art Dept.

Broken Trust

By Anonymous

When I first arrived at my residential treatment center, I really needed a friend, someone to speak to, and Sam was the first staff I came in contact with. Soon we were treating each other like brother and sister.

Sometimes, for breakfast, Sam would bring me hash browns from Burger King. When I was sick he would bring me home-made soup his mother made for me. We'd hang out a lot, joking on other people or on each other.

Sam was the first adult I told I was lesbian. Sam told me about his relationships, too. He told me he was married, but that he had a significant other besides his spouse. He showed me pictures. He told me all about the things he went through.

My friendship with Sam was important to me, because before Sam I was never really close to a man in my life. Growing up, I had been molested repeatedly since age 3, so it was hard for me to be close to an older guy in the first place. With Sam I felt different.

Then one night "my dog" Jennifer told me something I couldn't believe. I was chilling in her room. Out the window I saw Sam getting ready to go home, so I screamed out, "Good night. Get home safe." He called back, "Thank you. Good night. Sweet dreams."

When I looked back, Jennifer was looking sort of sad, so I asked, "What's wrong?"

She said, "You promise me you won't say nothing?"

I said, "Yes, I promise you."

Then she told me to sit down. She said, "Remember the night Sam came and got me from AWOL?"

I said, "Yeah." I was trying to figure out what she was going to tell me but I couldn't figure it out.

"Well, he did catch me," she said, "and then we did the nasty in the bushes."

I said to myself, "What the hell is she telling me? Sam would not do a thing like that." But she kept going.

"Yeah," she said. "We kept on kissing, then he was feeling on me."

I couldn't believe it. I was thinking, "Why would he want you? You're young and immature, and you still have the body of a little girl." Jennifer was only 14 at the time and Sam was in his early 30s. But I didn't say any of that. Instead, I kept a straight face and told her to go on.

Jennifer told me that she had feelings for Sam and wanted a relationship with him. In the end I convinced her that she shouldn't, mainly because she already had a girlfriend on campus, and I was relieved that she listened to me. But I also felt hurt and betrayed by Sam. Even though Jennifer liked Sam and said she wasn't sorry she'd been with him, what Sam did was wrong. Jennifer was still a child and Sam was a grown man being paid to take care of her.

Besides, since we lived at a residential treatment center where we didn't have a lot of freedom and were far away from our homes, we were all stuck on campus without too much outside support. The only people we had to rely on were each other and staff. Lots of times that made the girls even more anxious to win staff's approval. Staff had a lot of influence over some of the girls, but Sam abused his position of authority and trust.

At that moment I felt like Sam was just like the guys who had molested me, betrayed my trust, and taken advantage of me when I was vulnerable. I wondered if I could trust anyone. My heart sank to the floor.

I was thinking, "Why would he want you? You're young and immature, and you still have the body of a little girl."

When I saw Sam after that I felt weird being with him, but I didn't show it. I didn't stop being close to him and I didn't ask him any questions, because he was the one person who was the most there for me. I didn't want to be stuck on campus without Sam's support. Besides, I'd told Jennifer I would keep her secret.

Still, after what Jennifer told me, Sam and I started to argue a lot. On some days I'd call him names. He thought I was just joking but I wasn't. Then the next day we'd be best friends again. On the days we were best friends, I would think how glad I was that he was there for me. But on the days that we argued, I saw all the molesters who I'd ever come in contact with. I saw them pretending that everything was fine when it wasn't. Sam pretended that everything was all right, too, like he didn't do anything at all.

I felt more confused than ever about whom I could trust, and especially whether I should trust Sam. He stayed on our campus for a few more months and then left for his own reasons. But what he did has continued to affect me. I haven't really gotten close to any male staff member since then, and I don't feel like I can trust men in general, either. I believe that's partly because of how Sam's actions affected me.

Unfortunately, Sam wasn't the only staff who saw the girls on our campus as easy booty. Seven or eight months after Sam left, a new staff came. I really didn't pay him any mind until one of the girls came to me and said she'd gone to his house and had sex with him.

Robert was in his late 20s and the girl was 15 at the time. She gave me lots of details about where he lived. So the next week, when another girl came to me and said she'd had sex with him too, I asked her a couple of questions to see if she described his house the same way. She broke it down to a T.

I asked both of them if they would do it again and they said yes. One of them said she even had sex with him in her own cottage. Even though both girls said they wanted to be with him, I still felt the same way I'd felt about Jennifer and Sam: that Robert was taking advantage of his position as a caretaker and of their trust and vulnerabilities. He was teaching them that the only way they'd get love from anyone was by having sex, and that's a lesson too many of us first learned when we were sexually abused.

Soon other girls seemed to be involved with Robert. Sometimes the girls he was dealing with would get upset. They'd seem down if he wasn't around or if he was ignoring them or trying to break it off with them. They'd get mad and yell at him or try to attack him. Two girls started fighting over him. The staff just thought they were having personality differences, but the residents knew the real reason.

Then one day one of the girls who had a crush on him decided to tell. She told the administration and they held a meeting. But by the time the meeting came it was too late. The girl who told had run away.

After that the administration dropped it, but then some of the other staff started their own investigation. They asked the girls more about what Robert did or what he said, and a lot of girls who'd been involved with him told staff what had been going on.

Staff found out that he typically offered to meet the girls at his house. So they asked the girls who had been with him what his house looked like, so they could be sure they were telling the truth. They gave them all the same details they had given me, from what was across the street, to the doorman, to the way his living room was set up.

After that, some staff went to the administration about it and again another meeting was called. But it seemed like lots of the girls were confused about what they wanted to happen. Although they'd told the staff about Robert, they weren't willing to tell their stories in front of the administration. I guess some of them still had feelings for him, and others probably didn't want to stand up in public and get him in trouble.

But I decided that this time it was going to be different with me. Unlike with Sam and all the men who'd molested me, this time I decided to speak up about what was happening. My staff asked me if I would tell the administration what I had heard and I agreed. I felt like I needed to speak up for all the other girls who didn't speak up for themselves.

When it came time for the meeting I had a case of sweaty palms, but when I told what I knew I felt kind of strong. I hadn't stood up to the people who molested me when I was a child because I was too young to know that it was wrong, but this time I could do something about it. I felt strong for standing up for the other girls.

I told all that I had heard and I really expected him to get fired. But they didn't fire him. About a week after the meeting, they just transferred Robert to a boys' group home.

I don't know why they did that. Maybe they didn't want to report him because then the whole agency would look bad. Or maybe they felt they just didn't have enough evidence against him. But if that's the case, I really don't think they tried hard enough, because I think there was plenty of evidence if they really wanted to find it.

For instance, if they'd been willing to press charges against him and have a judge order that the other girls talk, I don't think the girls would have continued to deny their stories. But that would have been a lot of embarrassment for the agency.

Moving him to the boys' campus didn't really keep him away from the girls on our campus, because he still got to see them through the parties and picnics that the boys' and girls' group homes have together. And if he was sleeping with the girls on our campus, it's possible he would sleep with the boys, too.

After I found out that there weren't any serious consequences for Robert, I felt I had spoken up for nothing and questioned whether I'd done the right thing. My emotions told me that I was right, that someone had to do something to try to stop all this molesting. But after I left the campus to live in a group home, I heard that another staff came and had sexual relations with some of the girls. That upset me.

I've met some good people at my agency, but this makes me feel that my agency thinks anyone can take care of us, since we're just kids in foster care. All kids in the system have some sort of problems from their pasts, so some people may think it's no big deal to dump more problems on us. But I think it's hard enough to deal with what's already been dealt us. To pick up another bad card once we're in care is too much to take.

There should be higher standards for the staff who work with us. And agencies should train staff better after they've been hired. Staff members should know that sleeping with residents is a violation of their responsibilities and that there will be serious consequences for doing it. That way they'll think twice before jeopardizing our trust and their jobs.

I also think drastic measures should be taken once the agency gets information that something like this is going on. When it does happen, I think it's the agency's responsibility to dead it before it goes too far. They should send a message by firing staff or even by pressing charges. They shouldn't just sweep it under the rug because they're afraid it will embarrass them.

Patricia Battles

Taming My Anger

By Tray T.

At my group home they called me Cupcakes. They took my things and threw water in my face. Once, when I was asleep, a boy urinated in a cup and threw it on my covers. Another time, a boy set my bed on fire when I wasn't there, then he and four other kids jumped me. I beat them up and trashed their rooms.

Being in foster care is hard. But being gay in foster care takes the struggle to a whole new level. Anger became my weapon against those who antagonized me, but over time I came to realize that my anger also threatened to destroy me.

My angry ways began long before, when I was a child. My mother did drugs, and she'd leave my younger brother, sister, and me alone. Or she'd take us to our aunt's house, where my older male cousins sexually abused me. They told me not to tell anyone and that if I did, they would do it again.

For a long time I felt like everyone was out to hurt me. Because of my mom's neglect and the horrible things my cousins did to me, I felt no one loved me. I kept that inside for a long time, until it turned into rage.

When I was seven I was put in foster care, but that didn't stop my anger. In my first foster home I got into an argument with my foster mom over my long hair. She said that it was feminine. I said I didn't give a damn.

Later that night she came into my room while I was asleep and cut my hair. The next morning when I saw my hair on my pillow, I went off. I got a broom, went to her room, and hit her in her sleep. Then I destroyed her living room. For the next five years, I never lived in one foster home longer than a few months.

When I started living in group homes, I tried hard to keep the other boys from finding out that I was gay. After I beat up the boys who had called me Cupcakes, the staff felt I was in danger so they moved me to another group home. Things didn't get any better.

I got restrained several times a month for fighting. With my temper and weighing almost 300 pounds, it took five or six staff to pin me.

But after a while, I started secretly going out with a guy I liked. It got around to the staff, and my therapist told me about GLASS (Gay and Lesbian Adolescent Social Services), which is for gay and lesbian foster kids in Los Angeles.

I was tired of kids calling me names and trying to fight me because I was gay, so I agreed to go to GLASS. I thought I was going to do good. But I didn't realize I would have to get used to a new environment and new people all over again.

When I first went to GLASS I was the old Trayvione again. Kids knew not to mess with me when I gave my look—rolling my eyes and raising my lip. The whole room would clear when I was going to get into a fight. The staff would have to pull me off. Sometimes I liked being the person people were scared of. I had control—or so I thought.

Then one day, after I'd been at GLASS about six months, a staff person made me think about things in a new way.

She told us that when she was younger she'd imagined different ways she might end up, like being a prostitute, robbing people, or being homeless. Then she imagined herself working with kids and realized that's what she wanted to do with her life.

It made me imagine my own future. I imagined myself hurting somebody and ending up in jail. I imagined myself on the streets. That made me want to change.

Around the same time, my social worker was getting fed up with me. He told the staff that if anything else happened, to call the police and take me to jail. I was pissed off, but I was also scared. It was time to straighten up.

But it was hard to change because being angry was all I knew how to be. I took baby steps. I went to therapy. I also found someone I could trust.

Her name was Isabelle and she was one of the group home staff. One time I got in an argument with her. She wouldn't back down. She said, "I can see something in you. I know you can go far and I'm going to help you." I started going to her when something made me angry.

I felt no one loved me. I kept that inside for a long time, until it turned into rage.

I also started to accept that I was gay. When I arrived at GLASS I didn't know there were young people who were openly gay. It was weird seeing gay people who were acting feminine and flamboyant.

I had always known I was gay, but I didn't want to admit it. I realized that GLASS was where I belonged, where I could be open and not be made fun of.

One day I said, "I'm gay." The kids said, "Girl, we already knew." I busted out wearing a rainbow belt.

Being able to be myself made me happier. I made friends. I started listening to the staff's suggestions for ways to keep calm.

When I was mad I'd count to 10, dance in my room, or sit in a chair and listen to my CD player, bobbing my head to the music. Or I'd ignore the person and talk to staff or my friends. I signed up for art and dancing groups.

I still had my ups and downs. One time I went off on a staff at my group home because she didn't know how to cook. Isabelle overheard and pulled me out of the kitchen. We talked about it. I was getting older and I saw I couldn't do these things anymore.

When I was 15 I moved to another group home at GLASS. I became friends with one of the girls, Tiffany. She was the only person to stand up to me, which made me respect her. We talked about relationships and stuff in our lives, and I knew Tiffany wasn't going to give up on me.

One time I got in an argument with Isabelle. She wouldn't back down.

Everything was going real good. Then, on my 16th birthday, I went to my mother's house and my cousin tried to molest me again. I told him I wasn't a child anymore and was big enough and old enough to defend myself, so he backed off.

When I came back I told my therapist. It was the first time I'd told someone about what happened to me. I knew that if I wanted to get somewhere, it had to start now. Talking about it made me less angry.

I was voted president of the Resident Advisory Board, a group that plans fun activities. In June we set up an open mike. Me, Tiffany, and another girl in our house did a dance routine to hip-hop and R&B.

We laughed and played around as we practiced in the living room, each of us throwing our own moves in. I love dancing because it makes me feel like I'm not vulnerable. It puts me in a place where I'm far away and free.

I sometimes visit my brother and sister, who got adopted. But I have no contact with my mom. It's too much pain.

GLASS is my family now. I feel loved. The staff makes me feel like I always have someone to talk to. I know they expect more out of me. It makes me want to do good because I know I will let them down if I mess up.

I still argue and get upset, but I don't go off. When I see other kids acting like beasts—destroying things, fighting, yelling at staff, and not listening—I see myself. It's a trip because I think, "Damn, I did that."

Some days it still gets me mad that I felt that pain from my cousins, two people who were supposed to love me. But then I think of all the things I went through and I thank God I got through it. I've learned how to deal with my anger in ways that aren't self-destructive, and what I went through is now making me stronger.

The author is a writer for LA Youth, a paper for and by teens. Copyright © LA Youth. Reprinted with permission.

Marc Mazurkiewicz

Goodbye, Again!

By Giselle John

I've been in foster care for almost 16 months now and have come across many people who have helped me deal with the various problems I've faced. One of those persons is my present case-worker, Naomi, who did her very best to show me that I was someone valuable, with a purpose in this life.

But Naomi is the second caseworker I've had (and the third person from my agency) who I came to love, who then left the agency.

Pat, my first caseworker, left so suddenly that I didn't have a chance to say goodbye. I remember clearly the first time I met Pat. It was at Family Court. She came as a representative from the agency on my behalf. The encounter was so weird to me. I didn't know what she looked like, yet when I saw this tall, dark, slim young lady pass down the hall, looking as if she was lost, I said to her, "Excuse me, but is your name Patricia Phillips?"

"Yes," she answered.

"Well, my name is Giselle John."

"Oh," she said, "then it's you I'm looking for."

We laughed at the fact that I randomly picked her out from everyone else in the hallway. We then sat in the courtroom getting acquainted and talking about my case while we waited to appear before the judge.

I also remember clearly when Pat left. First she was changed from being my caseworker. I was upset when I found out. I didn't care to meet my new caseworker, Naomi Sunshine. "What a name," I thought to myself when I first heard it.

It hurt me very much to lose Pat as my caseworker. I cried, because I had become so attached to her and she had become my friend. We always had something in common. She was from the Caribbean, just like I was. We always talked about the West Indies. Pat was from Jamaica and I was from Trinidad and Tobago, so we could both relate to what life in the Caribbean was like.

Soon after being switched as my caseworker, Pat left the agency. It happened so fast. One minute she was here and the next she was gone without a trace.

The last time I saw Pat was when she accompanied my new caseworker, Naomi, to my home, so that they could take me to the hospital for an evaluation. They both knew that I would not go easily. I was being taken for an evaluation because the day before I wanted my life to end. I didn't want to live another day with the hurt I was feeling. The nightmares and painful memories of my past just would not go away. I wanted to die, so I could be put out of my misery.

Pat convinced me that I should go to the hospital because of the way I was feeling. Unfortunately, my visit to the hospital lasted four days.

When I was released from the hospital, Naomi came to pick

me up without Pat, so I asked, "Where is Pat?" Then Naomi said she had something to tell me.

"Giselle," she said, "Pat doesn't work with us anymore. The day after you came to the hospital, she left the next morning."

"Why?" I asked.

"I don't know," she replied.

My heart sank and tears rolled down my cheeks. I couldn't believe it—just like that Pat was gone. For a long time, whenever I went to the agency, I hoped I would see Pat sitting at her desk.

I finally got around to accepting Naomi. She showed that she was genuinely concerned about my well-being. She worked hard to solve any

Just like that, Pat was gone. For a long time, whenever I went to the agency, I hoped I would see Pat sitting at her desk.

problem I faced, even though sometimes I felt that she didn't listen to what I had to say. She was sometimes able to convince me that she understood me.

Naomi and I have had our problems, but we've been able to work them out with time. She's stuck with me when I went through rough times. She knew how sad I was when Pat and then Trudy, the education coordinator, left.

I had become very fond of Trudy. It was a pleasure to know her, and I felt sad when after a workshop one Thursday afternoon she announced that she was leaving.

"Again?" I asked myself. "Another one again?" When Trudy left I remembered Pat—how she left so suddenly and how much it hurt. I promised myself that I wouldn't get so close to anyone anymore. I didn't want to feel hurt when they left.

I even mentioned to Naomi that I was afraid that she would leave also and that it would hurt me a great deal. She then said that she wasn't going anywhere soon, and I believed her.

Several months later, Naomi took me to see the doctor, then we stopped at a restaurant to get something to eat. While we were eating, she said to me, "Giselle, I have something to tell you, and I don't know how. All day I've been trying to think of a way to say it to you, but I can't find one, so I'll just say it. I'm leaving the agency in a couple of weeks."

Immediately I turned my eyes away from her. In my mind all I could say was, "I knew it." I couldn't cry, because I was more angry at her than sad. She said we could talk about it, but I refused. I tried to ignore her, but I couldn't. The bottom line was that she was leaving, and I would have to get a new caseworker all over again.

Seeing Naomi at the agency for the last time was very painful. I just couldn't get over the fact that she wasn't going to be there anymore. I couldn't deal with saying goodbye to her, but I had to.

As I was waiting to collect my stipend after the workshop, Naomi asked if she could speak to me and I agreed. She wanted to let me know how she felt about saying goodbye to me, but that just wasn't enough. I wanted her to tell me that she was going to be around a little longer, but instead she was telling me how bad she felt. As she spoke tears streamed down my face. I felt as if my heart sank deep inside me and I could hardly talk. Tears mixed with anger took over my words. I had to accept the fact that she was really leaving and that this was goodbye.

I promised myself that I wouldn't get so close to anyone anymore. I didn't want to feel hurt when they left.

Naomi once told me that she wasn't leaving the agency soon and that she'd be around. But I wouldn't hold anything against her, because situations do change the direction our lives take, and this is what happened. Something came up in her life and she had to leave.

I know I'm going to miss her just like I missed Pat and Trudy. I've never gotten accustomed to saying goodbye, even though I've said it numerous times. I'll never forget the times we spent working with each other, working things out. Naomi is a good caseworker and I hope that the next caseworker I get will be as understanding and patient with me as she was. I will miss her, there's no doubt about that.

Giselle went on to graduate from college and run
Voices of Youth, a public speaking and advocacy organization
for teens in foster care.

Joshua Hector

A Safe Place

By Donalay Thomas

When I arrived at Rodney Street, a big brownstone group home, the staff accepted me in a way my own mother never did.

My mom, who adopted me when I was five months old, never accepted my sexuality. She raised me in a strong church background and always said things like, "Donalay, you can't serve two masters!" (By this she meant I couldn't like God and women.)

Eventually I got put in a residential treatment center where my peers abused me. The staff didn't protect me. One time I woke up in the hospital after a boy hit me in the head with a 20-pound weight, which left me with a seizure condition. My life was a living despair.

At Rodney Street I finally learned what it feels like to be free, to breathe in possibilities.

I knew right off the bat that Rodney Street was all about respect. When I got there, two staff asked if I was hungry. I noticed a smell I hadn't smelled in a while—home cooked food.

Then this one staff, who had a short haircut and male clothing, asked me, "Would you like to be called 'he?' If so, what's your male name?" I said I was fine being a she. Then this person said he wanted to be called "he" and that his name was Ryan.

The residents there made me welcome, too. I came to Rodney Street from a detention center. One resident who had been upstate knew I had probably arrived without clothes and asked me, "Yo, fam—you got clothes to wear?"

She gave me some of her clothes and told me I could keep them until I got some of my own. All the kids in the house seemed friendly and wanted to know what I was about.

Then I met my program manager, Danny. He's a gay man but is like a mother to me. He's there whenever I need a friend or parental guidance. He understands how lost I feel and has helped me find my way.

By listening to me and encouraging my writing, Danny has shown me how to take down the wall of my anger, brick by brick. He also praises me. "Donalay, your writing puts me to tears," he'll tell me. Before, I never believed in talking to someone else about my pain. But I can even talk to Danny about my love interests and how to handle being attracted to another resident.

After I moved in I decided I didn't like one staff, Shonda. She reminded me of my mother. But then Shonda surprised me.

When I called my mother to wish her a happy Valentine's Day, my mother mentioned that she had just returned from my godmother's burial. No one in my family had told me my godmother had died!

I believed I wasn't told because no one wanted me to show up at her wake in my best black male suit, sharp tie, and sexy male shoes. No one wanted to see me as I was—a masculine-looking lesbian. I was so hurt in so many ways all at once.

I told Shonda I was upset that my mother didn't tell me about my godmother's death in time for me to go to the funeral. "Since you remind me of my mother, can you give me a reason she would do something like this?" I asked.

"Donalay, your mother has her issues surrounding your sexuality," said Shonda. "You may realize that pleasing others will mean you can't please yourself. You may have to let go of your mother until you get your heart and mind intact."

Shonda made me think about how my mother refuses to acknowledge how much she hurts me. Because I want my mother's love and acceptance, she still has the power to make me feel bad about my sexuality. Shonda helped me build myself up to get past all the sadness and hurt I feel because my mother rejects me.

By listening to me and encouraging my writing, Danny has shown me how to take down the wall of my anger, brick by brick.

One day I was in front of my group home when my mother drove up and asked me to come over to the car. I was scared that she saw me smoking a cigarette with two other residents and would be mad, but I went over to her. My mother's eyes went right to the rainbow pride beads of my bracelet. She snatched them right off. I looked down as they skittled to the ground.

"You think I don't know what this means, Donalay?" My mother was angry. "You can't live with one foot in the door of God's house and one foot out."

"Why can't you understand and love me for me?" I asked. "Why can't you be my mother? Why do you have to be my critic?"

She drove off. My pride lay on the ground while my tears fell. I was embarrassed that she spewed her hate in front of my housemates. I felt angry, ashamed, and insulted.

Danny helped me deal with my mother's rejection. "Donalay, let it go," he said.

To have such a wonderful person in my life and to have such a caring staff team mean so much to me.

My mother used to tell me, "What doesn't kill you makes you stronger."

I'm stronger now, but not because my mother and other people have hurt me so badly. It's because I now have people who are here for me, and who accept me for who I am.

Donalay wrote this story when she was 17.

Martell Brown

One Tough Mama

By Tashara Gilyard

Bernadetta Hayward is a senior childcare worker who has been working in a group home in New York City for 13 years. I thought she might have a good perspective on how staff and kids relate in the system. Bernadetta talked to me about what rules work in a group home and what rules don't work. I think that the boys in Bernadetta's group home are lucky to have her in their lives. I also think some other group home staff could learn from her example.

Q: I'm sure residents complain about the rules in your house. When do you discuss their concerns and when do you just say, "That's tough, but those are the rules?"

A: We have our rap sessions, or what I call our Indian teepees. We sit on the floor Indian style with food all around us. If we're having an issue, I'll ask them, "What do you think is fair?" and we'll negotiate. I tell them, "If you want to make this like a family, you've got to help me make the rules. But if you do and you break them, there are going to be consequences." Usually the consequences are, they'll lose part of their curfew or phone privileges. Or if they have a single room, they could lose that.

If I put a kid on restriction, he has to come to me to negotiate if he feels it's unfair. But I don't change my punishment too often because first they have to prove to me that they've changed their behavior. When I'm too hard on a kid and I realize it, then I do apologize. Just like in all families, people make mistakes and you have to be able to apologize. It helps.

Q: When kids get in trouble, sometimes after-school activities are taken away. But being stuck in the house can make kids act even worse. Is this something you do?

A: I would never take away any after-school program. That's teaching, and I would never interfere with teaching. But if there's an agency trip they really want to go on and they do something drastic, maybe I would take that away.

Q: When do you use restraints and why?

A: We have not used restraints in a long time. Physical restraints, or holding a kid when he's getting violent, is not meant to hurt a child but to calm a behavior down. Restraints should be done with the minimum force and the maximum love. But physical restraint should be the last thing you ever do. You should only use them if a child is physically harming himself or another person. And sometimes restraints can hype a child up and make things worse, so you really need to be careful.

Q: How do you think kids can be helped to succeed without making them feel like they're slaves to your rules?

A: I think that the city needs a better structure to hold kids responsible. Now when a kid decides he's not going to get up and go to school that day or he's not going for months, there's very little we can do. But the city has an abundance of money, and they should develop programs to deal with what's really going on with the kids. When kids aren't doing anything, it's because they're scared and they're not waking up to reality. They're scared to go to school and they're scared of the future.

When I'm too hard on a kid and I realize it, then I do apologize. Just like in all families, people make mistakes.

One idea I have is for the city to build halfway houses for kids who aren't going to school or will not work. They would put GED programs or work-training programs into these homes. This would make it easier for kids to get over their fears. Once they're more on track, they could go back into the group home.

In the meantime, sometimes staff members just have to stay on kids' cases, even if the kids don't like that. We had a kid who refused to go to school, to go to work, or do anything. So we had a child welfare specialist talk to him and keep him motivated. And I've stayed on his case, too. Sometimes I'll spend three or four hours talking to him about going to school. But sometimes I do get fed up and just say, "Enough is enough. You're going."

Tashara was 18 when she conducted this interview.

Marcus Pierno

A Three-Point Shooter

By Max Moran

You know what's the worst part of living in a group home? I'll tell you. It's getting based on points. In other words, if I'm a good boy I get the right amount of points. But if I'm a naughty kid, I get a big fat "0" on my point sheet. If I get zeros, it means that I will not get no more than $2 for allowance, and nowadays $2 is barely enough for two condoms.

Or maybe the worst part is the food. I mean it seems like we eat the same thing every other day. Macaroni and cheese and chicken, and sometimes I can see the redness in the chicken. I got a strong stomach, but this sight makes me wanna throw up. I just go to my room, blast my favorite CD, take a shower, and go to sleep on an empty stomach.

No, I know what's the worst part. It's the fact that most of our counselors are not able to fulfill their duties. One counselor who works on weekends, all he does is sleep on the couch all day until it's time for him to go home. Another talks on the phone all night long and another loves arguing. And I love arguing, too. It helps me get rid of all that frustration.

Oh yeah! Let me tell you about my senior counselor. All she does is sit her behind in her chair and do nothing. Whenever we need something, it always takes her so long to get it for us. She forgets things a lot. I remember one time she forgot to cook dinner. She's a very good person at heart, but she's just not helping us enough.

I do admit that there are one or two counselors who are real cool. There's one who I can talk to about anything, on any level. He can be serious and funny at the same time. I'll call him Jim.

One time I was watching TV and Jim turned the TV off because everybody else didn't do their chores. I just went crazy. I threw the chair I was sitting in all the way across the living room and went upstairs to my room and blasted my radio. My senior counselor was right there when this happened, yet she didn't come to speak to me.

I can't believe she didn't have five minutes to speak to me. I'm not even worth five minutes? Soon Jim came to my room and started to talk to me. I just told him that all I wanted to do was watch TV. I mean, this summer I'm working basically all day long. If I can't come home to a decent hot meal, at least let me watch TV. Soon Jim apologized and we gave each other a pound and everything was chill.

Maybe the worst part of living in a group home is that we only get $120 for clothing money, and on top of that the check is always two months late. Maybe the most humiliating thing is that we have a pay phone in the kitchen which sometimes doesn't take quarters, so we can only take incoming calls.

There are so many things wrong in this house. When I get time to cook something, I have to go through hell because the stove doesn't always work. Maybe the thing that gets on my nerves the most is that this resident is on the phone with like five different girls. The sad part about it is that he doesn't get any. Any other crazy kid in here would have gotten some from all five of those girls. Sometimes I feel like killing him just for some phone time. I'm a very quiet person, but I guess really bad persons are the quiet type.

Maybe the worst part of living here is that I'm going through a great depression and yet none of the counselors seem to care.

Or maybe the worst part of living here is that I'm going through a great depression and yet none of the counselors seem to care. When I'm sad, all I do is sit outside my house on the steps and just cry. I put my hands over my face so people that pass by won't see me crying.

Other times I go to my backyard with a basketball in my hand and just shoot three-pointers. The longer the distance I shoot from, the better. I always make things hard on myself. That's how my life has been to this day. I'm always trying to shoot three-pointers when I should be making layups. God knows I shoot so many airballs, but someday I'll be a good three-point shooter. Someday.

After graduating from college, Max earned an MSW from Hunter College and became a social worker.

Beatrice Bass

Me and My Mentor

By Tara Bonaparte

It was very hard when I was first placed in a foster care residential treatment center (RTC). I was full of anger and ready to take it out on the world. I really needed someone to talk to so that I could sort out the hidden issues behind my round face and pretty smile.

The thing that got me confused was that even though I was an angry child, I knew that I wasn't the only angry child on that whole campus. But as I looked around, I saw that they weren't really upset or they didn't seem to be thinking the same angry thoughts that I was. These children went through the same problems that I went through, but they didn't seem as affected as I was. What made them seem to be a little bit more happier than me?

My mother and father always told me about the Tooth Fairy

and Santa Claus. They told me about Superman and Batman and all the other things that possess the powers to make children happy.

But they never told me about the best hero ever invented. They never told me about the people who have the power to make every child they encounter happy. These people aren't make believe. They go by the name of "mentor."

I never knew about mentors until one day when I was very upset. I was crying in my room because I missed being at home and talking to my parents. So one of my cottage mates came into my room and told me that she would talk to me after she came back from going out with her mentor. I asked her what a mentor was and she told me.

A mentor is someone who can be a positive role model in your life. Someone who takes on the role of being a big sister or brother. In some cases they even take on the role of your mother and father.

A mentor is someone you can talk to when you need to spill out your soul. And you never have to worry about your mentor never being there. My experience with my mentor helped me see past the negative.

Every time I looked around St. Christopher's, all I saw were children with their mentors. I saw children going on home visits with their mentors. Children going shopping with their mentors. And I felt really left out.

And the more I looked, the more I realized that I wanted a mentor too. So I was left in a bind. And day by day I was becoming more and more upset. Until…

I had to be driven every Monday to see my sisters. And I used to have a regular driver who took me every week. But for some reason they told him that he couldn't drive me anymore.

So they asked a crisis team worker named Karen Smith to drive me. I still was mad about not having my regular driver, but I found myself telling my whole life story to Karen, a person

What Foster Care Staff Need to Know

I barely knew.

Soon Karen became my regular driver. Every week I would look forward to going to see my sisters so that I could talk to Karen and she could give me the advice that I needed. And surprisingly, I took the words she used and made them useful in my life.

I soon found myself really caring for Karen like she was one of my family members. And for the first time in a long time, I found someone who cared for me too. Karen is someone I had to meet in order to finally trust again.

I was full of anger and ready to take it out on the world. I really needed someone to talk to.

But I tried to not let her know that I really wanted her to be my mentor, because of a previous situation I'd been in. I really started to like this one lady who used to work in my cottage. But when she got moved to another cottage, she forgot about me and became the mentor for another kid. After that, I didn't want a mentor.

But finally I spilled the beans. And the caring from Karen didn't stop. In fact, she really started cracking down on me HARD.

Karen always made sure that I did my best in everything. And whenever she got the chance, she always took the time to talk to me and to tell me right from wrong. I felt that even when she was not around, she was still looking over me. And I gave Karen the title not only of my "mentor" but of "my conscience."

Every time I was about to do wrong, I heard Karen telling me what I needed to hear and setting me straight. And I felt her pushing me in the direction of where I needed to go. (Not actually pushing me, but you know what I mean.)

And every time I did something good and ran to tell her, Karen said "Good." Now, to someone else, that would mean nothing, but to me that meant a lot.

But there was one thing that started to bother me about my

96

relationship with Karen.

O n my campus there is a tradition between mentors and mentees. It's called "the scarf swap," which means that your mentor has to buy you a scarf when he or she feels that you are doing really good.

Every time I saw a girl in my cottage walking around with a scarf given to her by her mentor, it made me feel really upset. Sometimes I felt that I should just go up to Karen and ask her, "What is up with the scarf!?!"

But I also felt that I shouldn't. I felt that when Karen thought that I deserved a scarf, I would be very happy with the scarf that she gave me. But when would that be?

One day I wanted to go shopping, so I asked Karen to take me. Of course she said yes. And she took me to the mall. We did a lot of window shopping. We laughed at almost everything.

I picked out some things that I liked (with the help of Karen) and she bought me something to eat. Then, from across the street, there it was—staring me in the face. It was the most beautiful scarf I had ever seen.

I found myself telling my whole life story to Karen, a person I barely knew.

We finished eating and she took me into that store. I picked up the scarf and walked around the store with it. Karen looked at me and told me to put the scarf on the counter. Then she paid for it. YES! I finally had my mentor scarf.

When I walked back in the cottage, it was like I had a special glow to me. When everyone saw me with my scarf, I was bombarded with questions. And when all the other girls who had been through the scarf swap found out, it was like I was invited to join a special underground club.

I felt mad important and that made me walk around with better self-esteem. So not only did getting a mentor make me feel more accepted by my peers, I felt better accepted by myself.

I can honestly say that having Karen Smith as a mentor did a lot of good for me. She helped me to change myself in a lot of ways. She helped me educationally, because she always made sure I was in school. She helped me mentally, because she was always there when I thought I was about to lose my mind. And she was there emotionally, because she always took my feelings seriously. These are the things I needed in my life so I wouldn't flip. And I think that without Ms. Karen Smith, my life would definitely be something you hear about on "America's Most Wanted."

The best advice that I could possibly give would be to get a mentor. A mentor could be a family member that you look up to, a teacher, or anybody. Having a mentor helped me fit one more missing piece into the puzzle of my life.

Tara was 15 when she wrote this story.

Marcus Pierno

A New Beginning

By Mohamed Khan

There was always a wall between me and other people, stopping me from speaking out or mingling with my peers. Unlike a normal kid my age, I never hung out with anyone. Come to think of it, I didn't even have one close friend. From school to my apartment, and that was all. But then I moved into a totally new world by going into care.

I used to live in a quiet neighborhood. There were hardly any stores in my area and there weren't many people in the streets. My family's apartment was a simple yet cozy place for my two older brothers, 20 and 25, my mother, my father, and me.

While my second brother and I shared a room, my oldest brother had his own room right next to ours. That left my mother and father, who slept in a little portion of the living room.

I went into the system when I was 15. The group home that I

was placed into was the total opposite of my family's apartment, in both size and neighborhood. The shift to a whole new setting was one that started to change my life forever.

Unlike my old neighborhood, this new area was packed with people morning, noon, and night. This made me feel as if the whole world was crashing in on me. Everywhere I looked, there were people. This definitely wasn't like my old neighborhood. This would have been a good thing if I wasn't so obsessed with being alone.

The sub-level of the group home, I recall, consisted of a laundry room and an enormous hangout room with a television and seats for four. This floor alone was about two-thirds as big as my old apartment.

There was also a fairly big first floor and an even larger second floor. There were five bedrooms upstairs, any of which could make my room at home look puny. This group home was at least two and a half times the size of my old apartment.

As I previously stated, I was a quiet kid before I went into the system. Many knew me, but never spoke to me, I guess because I always had an "air" around me that said I wanted to be alone.

I wouldn't bother with the after-school ruckus involving sports or girl watching. That wasn't my thing. Many days I preferred to just go home and do nothing. I would find comfort in not having to listen to anyone else or try to impress anyone.

With no one else around, I made the rules. I could do what I wanted and not "hear" the stares from people looking at me. I suppose I was a bit too self-conscious.

Then, in an instant, I was living with seven teenage boys and at least two supervisors. I didn't even know what a group home was at that time, nor did I want to. All that I knew for sure was that I was no longer alone.

Although I still kept to myself, my defensive wall began slowly crumbling. Living with strangers was not going to be easy.

It was not really the rules or the regulations that bothered me.

No, I had no problems there. The rules were actually very lenient, being that it was a home for first-time placements.

It was the lack of privacy that I could not stand. I couldn't retreat into my "world" anymore. There was no door on my bedroom, no locks on my closets or drawers, not even on the bathroom door. Nowhere for me to hide, which in turn meant I had no peace of mind.

I could be in the middle of a shower and "creeeek." "Oops, I didn't know you were in here." Or I could be in the middle of changing my clothes when an old female supervisor would walk into my bedroom.

I ran from everyone for as long as I could. No one would get into my world, no matter how hard they tried.

Faced by these changes, I was going through hell. "Who do these people think they are?" I thought. "Why is this happening to me?"

One thing I really hated were the Sunday trips our group home took together. Being forced to go along with people I didn't want to be with, to a place I didn't want to go, when I just wanted to be alone. This is how I felt, not just on Sundays, but every day.

I remember one trip we took to the Brooklyn Bridge. It was a walk across the bridge for a charity event. "Wear comfortable shoes," said the supervisors, "and don't forget your shorts, it'll be a hot one."

"Does everyone have to go?" I asked.

"Yes, everyone must go together and stay together."

Great, now my torment would begin.

This was my first weekend at the group home, so I did everything that I was told without question. I didn't want to seem like a trouble maker.

So, I went along quietly. As everyone got on the train, the anxiety began to build inside of me. I could feel the eyes looking at me, like I was the prey of hungry lions. It seemed as though every time I would build up enough courage to look at one person, there would be a whole group looking back.

Finally, we arrived at the bridge. When we got off the train we were told to stick together. I pretended to walk with a group of guys from the group home until we got to the bridge.

But less than two minutes into the walk I disappeared. I walked leisurely away from everyone else. I began to walk faster and faster. Before I knew it I was in a mini-sprint. Maybe deep down I was trying to run away from everybody.

I arrived at the end of the bridge long before anyone else. Once I did I simply sat down, put my head between my knees, and finally had some time alone.

We talked that morning for at least two hours. Without even knowing it, she came into my life and related so well.

Sure, there were people constantly passing back and forth, but I didn't care. I could finally just sit there and do nothing without anyone asking, "What's wrong with the new guy?" It was only a few minutes of being alone before everyone else arrived, but it kept me going.

After that, I decided to run from everyone for as long as I could. No one would get into my world, no matter how hard they tried.

But I did talk to six of the seven boys that I was living with. Your occasional hi's and bye's and small talk. They were all friendly. I was slightly older, so I guess they looked up to me a little. Sometimes I would go out to the store or to the park and, before I knew it, I had company. There were even times we got along really well, like best friends, but I never let them get too close.

They took it upon themselves to try to find out what was on my mind. All six of them tried to pry into my personal life. All six of them failed. There was no way I was going to let anyone get past my wall. Until one day when I got caught with my guard down.

A supervisor and I were having breakfast alone one day. No one else was awake yet. Then she suddenly asked, "Why are you here?" So I told her that I had family problems that I needed to get away from. Little did I know this would lead up to the single most important conversation that I had ever had.

Turns out, we talked that morning for at least two hours. Without even knowing it, she came into my life and related so well. For everything I told her, there was some sound, logical advice she had to give.

I let her know about the physical abuse that I had gone through at home. The supervisor simply replied, "Isn't that how your parents were brought up? Do you honestly think they hate you?"

I thought for a second and then I told her how it was affecting my school life negatively. She wisely replied again, "I know that there must be a lot on your mind. You should try talking about it more." Then she took a long, hard look at me and concluded: "That's what I'm here for."

So, the next day, I returned to her, asking for more advice. We talked again for what seemed like forever.

"Do you really think I belong in here?" I asked.

"No one really belongs in a group home," she said. "Just think of it as an interval to your next step in life."

By the end of our conversation, I felt the weirdest feeling I had ever had. It was a good, calm, "light" feeling. I couldn't understand why I felt like that because I had never had that feeling before. I knew that I liked it, though.

Before long, I figured it out. I tied together the feeling of inner tranquility to the casual conversations. Once I did, I began to speak a lot more often. I even got somewhat closer to the group home residents.

We all got along really well by the third and final week I was there. We went out together, played basketball, softball, and even hung out. We would sometimes go out at night and sit on the roof of the garage for an hour or so.

Although at first I didn't want to be friendly, I benefited greatly from the talking, playing, and joking around. It all helped in easing my tension.

I realized that I liked being spoken to and that I also liked to speak to others. Together with the help of the supervisors and my newly-made friends, I learned how to speak out and help others. By the time I left the group home three weeks later, these people had made such a positive impact on my life that I have a hard time describing it with words. This change continued on through the next 11 months, while I was living in a foster home.

For some, going into care can be heart-wrenching, even terrifying. However, if you handle it correctly and give in just a little, you'll be surprised at what can be accomplished. I would like to thank my foster care agency for giving me my new beginning.

Mohamed wrote this story when he was 17.

Townsend Press

Lost and Found

Darcy Wills winced at the loud rap music coming from her sister's room.

My rhymes were rockin'
MC's were droppin'
People shoutin' and hip-hoppin'
Step to me and you'll be inferior
'Cause I'm your lyrical superior.

Darcy went to Grandma's room. The darkened room smelled of lilac perfume, Grandma's favorite, but since her stroke Grandma did not notice it, or much of anything.

"Bye, Grandma," Darcy whispered from the doorway. "I'm going to school now."

Just then, the music from Jamee's room cut off, and Jamee rushed into the hallway.

The teen characters in the Bluford novels, a fiction series by Townsend Press, struggle with many of the same difficult issues as the writers in this book. Here's the first chapter from *Lost and Found*, by Anne Schraff, the first book in the series. In this novel, high school sophomore Darcy contends with the return of her long-absent father, the troubling behavior of her younger sister Jamee, and the beginning of her first relationship.

"Like she even hears you," Jamee said as she passed Darcy. Just two years younger than Darcy, Jamee was in eighth grade, though she looked older.

"It's still nice to talk to her. Sometimes she understands. You want to pretend she's not here or something?"

"She's not," Jamee said, grabbing her backpack.

"Did you study for your math test?" Darcy asked. Mom was an emergency room nurse who worked rotating shifts. Most of the time, Mom was too tired to pay much attention to the girls' schoolwork. So Darcy tried to keep track of Jamee.

"Mind your own business," Jamee snapped.

"You got two D's on your last report card," Darcy scolded. "You wanna flunk?" Darcy did not want to sound like a nagging parent, but Jamee wasn't doing her best. Maybe she couldn't make A's like Darcy, but she could do better.

Jamee stomped out of the apartment, slamming the door behind her. "Mom's trying to get some rest!" Darcy yelled. "Do you have to be so selfish?" But Jamee was already gone, and the apartment was suddenly quiet.

Darcy loved her sister. Once, they had been good friends. But now all Jamee cared about was her new group of rowdy friends. They leaned on cars outside of school and turned up rap music on their boom boxes until the street seemed to tremble like an earthquake. Jamee had even stopped hanging out with her old friend Alisha Wrobel, something she used to do every weekend.

Darcy went back into the living room, where her mother sat in the recliner sipping coffee. "I'll be home at 2:30, Mom," Darcy said. Mom smiled faintly. She was tired, always tired. And lately she was worried too. The hospital where she worked was cutting staff. It seemed each day fewer people were expected to do more work. It was like trying to climb a mountain that keeps getting taller as you go. Mom was forty-four, but just yesterday she said, "I'm like an old car that's run out of warranty, baby. You know what happens then. Old car is ready for the junk heap. Well, maybe that hospital is gonna tell me one of these days—'Mattie Mae Wills, we don't need you anymore. We can get somebody younger and cheaper.'"

"Mom, you're not old at all," Darcy had said, but they were only words, empty words. They could not erase the dark, weary lines from beneath her mother's eyes.

Darcy headed down the street toward Bluford High School. It was not a terrible neighborhood they lived in; it just was not good. Many front yards were not cared for. Debris—fast food wrappers, plastic bags, old newspapers—blew around and piled against fences and curbs. Darcy hated that. Sometimes she and other kids from school spent Saturday mornings cleaning up, but it seemed a losing battle. Now, as she walked, she tried to focus on small spots of beauty along the way. Mrs. Walker's pink and white roses bobbed proudly in the morning breeze. The Hustons' rock garden was carefully designed around a wooden windmill.

As she neared Bluford, Darcy thought about the science project that her biology teacher, Ms. Reed, was assigning. Darcy was doing hers on tidal pools. She was looking forward to visiting a real tidal pool, taking pictures, and doing research. Today, Ms. Reed would be dividing the students into teams of two. Darcy wanted to be paired with her close friend, Brisana Meeks. They were both excellent students, a cut above most kids at Bluford, Darcy thought.

"Today, we are forming project teams so that each student can gain something valuable from the other," Ms. Reed said as Darcy sat at her desk. Ms. Reed was a tall, stately woman who reminded Darcy of the Statue of Liberty. She would have been a perfect model for the statue if Lady Liberty had been a black woman. She never would have been called pretty, but it was possible she might have been called a handsome woman. "For this assignment, each of you will be working with someone you've never worked with before."

Darcy was worried. If she was not teamed with Brisana,

maybe she would be teamed with some really dumb student who would pull her down. Darcy was a little ashamed of herself for thinking that way. Grandma used to say that all flowers are equal, but different. The simple daisy was just as lovely as the prize rose. But still Darcy did not want to be paired with some weak partner who would lower her grade.

"Darcy Wills will be teamed with Tarah Carson," Ms. Reed announced.

Darcy gasped. Not Tarah! Not that big, chunky girl with the brassy voice who squeezed herself into tight skirts and wore lime green or hot pink satin tops and cheap jewelry. Not Tarah who hung out with Cooper Hodden, that loser who was barely hanging on to his football eligibility. Darcy had heard that Cooper had been left back once or twice and even got his driver's license as a sophomore. Darcy's face felt hot with anger. Why was Ms. Reed doing this?

Hakeem Randall, a handsome, shy boy who sat in the back row, was teamed with the class blabbermouth, LaShawn Appleby. Darcy had a secret crush on Hakeem since freshman year. So far she had only shared this with her diary, never with another living soul.

It was almost as though Ms. Reed was playing some devilish game. Darcy glanced at Tarah, who was smiling broadly. Tarah had an enormous smile, and her teeth contrasted harshly with her dark red lipstick. "Great," Darcy muttered under her breath.

Ms. Reed ord e red the teams to meet so they could begin to plan their projects.

As she sat down by Tarah, Darcy was instantly sickened by a syrupy-sweet odor.

She must have doused herself with cheap perfume this morning , Darcy thought.

"Hey, girl," Tarah said. "Well, don't you look down in the mouth. What's got you lookin' that way?"

It was hard for Darcy to meet new people, especially someone like Tarah, a person Aunt Charlotte would call "low class." These were people who were loud and rude. They drank too much, used drugs, got into fights and ruined the neighborhood. They yelled ugly insults at people, even at their friends. Darcy did not actually know that Tarah did anything like this personally, but she seemed like the type who did.

"I just didn't think you'd be interested in tidal pools," Darcy explained.

Tarah slammed her big hand on the desk, making her gold bracelets jangle like ice cubes in a glass, and laughed. Darcy had never heard a mule bray, but she was sure it made exactly the same sound. Then Tarah leaned close and whispered, "Girl, I don't know a tidal pool from a fool. Ms. Reed stuck us together to mess with our heads, you hear what I'm sayin'?"

"Maybe we could switch to other partners," Darcy said nervously.

A big smile spread slowly over Tarah's face. "Nah, I think I'm gonna enjoy this. You're always sittin' here like a princess collecting your A's. Now you gotta work with a regular person, so you better loosen up, girl!"

Darcy felt as if her teeth were glued to her tongue. She fumbled in her bag for her outline of the project. It all seemed like a horrible joke now. She and Tarah Carson standing knee-deep in the muck of a tidal pool!

"Worms live there, don't they?" Tarah asked, twisting a big gold ring on her chubby finger.

"Yeah, I guess," Darcy replied.

"Big green worms," Tarah continued. "So if you get your feet stuck in the bottom of that old tidal pool, and you can't get out, do the worms crawl up your clothes?"

Darcy ignored the remark. "I'd like for us to go there soon, you know, look around."

"My boyfriend, Cooper, he goes down to the ocean all the time. He can take us. He says he's seen these fiddler crabs. They look like big spiders, and they'll try to bite your toes off. Cooper says so," Tarah said.

"Stop being silly," Darcy shot back. "If you' re not even going to be serious . . . "

"You think you're better than me, don't you?" Tarah suddenly growled.

"I never said—" Darcy blurted.

"You don't have to say it, girl. It's in your eyes. You think I'm a low-life and you're something special. Well, I got more friends than you got fingers and toes together. You got no friends, and everybody laughs at you behind your back. Know what the word on you is? Darcy Wills give you the chills."

Just then, the bell rang, and Darcy was glad for the excuse to turn away from Tarah, to hide the hot tears welling in her eyes. She quickly rushed from the classroom, relieved that school was over. Darcy did not think she could bear to sit through another class just now.

Darcy headed down the long street towards home. She did not like Tarah. Maybe it was wrong, but it was true. Still, Tarah's brutal words hurt. Even stupid, awful people might tell you the truth about yourself. And Darcy did not have any real friends, except for Brisana. Maybe the other kids were mocking her behind her back. Darcy was very slender, not as shapely as many of the other girls. She remembered the time when Cooper Hodden was hanging in front of the deli with his friends, and he yelled as Darcy went by, "Hey, is that really a female there? Sure don't look like it. Looks more like an old broomstick with hair. " His companions laughed rudely, and Darcy had walked a little faster.

A terrible thought clawed at Darcy. Maybe she was the loser, not Tarah. Tarah was always hanging with a bunch of kids, laughing and joking. She would go down the hall to the lockers and greetings would come from everywhere. "Hey, Tarah!" "What's up, Tar?" "See ya at lunch, girl." When Darcy went to the lockers, there was dead silence.

Darcy usually glanced into stores on her way home from school. She enjoyed looking at the trays of chicken feet and pork ears at the little Asian grocery store. Sometimes she would even steal a glance at the diners sitting by the picture window at the Golden Grill Restaurant. But today she stared straight ahead, her shoulders drooping.

If this had happened last year, she would have gone directly to Grandma's house, a block from where Darcy lived. How many times had Darcy and Jamee run to Grandma's, eaten applesauce cookies, drunk cider, and poured out their troubles to Grandma. Somehow, their problems would always dissolve in the warmth of her love and wisdom. But now Grandma was a frail figure in the corner of their apartment, saying little. And what little she did say made less and less sense.

Darcy was usually the first one home. The minute she got there, Mom left for the hospital to take the 3:00 to 11:00 shift in the ER. By the time Mom finished her paperwork at the hospital, she would be lucky to be home again by midnight. After Mom left, Darcy went to Grandma's room to give her the malted nutrition drink that the doctor ordered her to have three times a day.

"Want to drink your chocolate malt, Grandma?" Darcy asked, pulling up a chair beside Grandma's bed.

Grandma was sitting up, and her eyes were open. "No. I'm not hungry," she said listlessly. She always said that.

"You need to drink your malt, Grandma," Darcy insisted, gently putting the straw between the pinched lips.

Grandma sucked the malt slowly. "Grandma, nobody likes me at school," Darcy said. She did not expect any response. But there was a strange comfort in telling Grandma anyway. "Everybody laughs at me. It's because I'm shy and maybe stuck-up, too, I guess. But I don't mean to be. Stuck-up, I mean. Maybe I'm weird. I could be weird, I guess. I could be like Aunt Charlotte . . ." Tears rolled down Darcy's cheeks. Her heart ached with loneliness. There was nobody to talk to anymore, nobody who had time to listen, nobody who understood.

Grandma blinked and pushed the straw away. Her eyes brightened as they did now and then. "You are a wonderful girl. Everybody knows that," Grandma said in an almost normal voice. It happened like that sometimes. It was like being in the middle of a dark storm and having the clouds part, revealing a patch of clear, sunlit blue. For just a few precious minutes, Grandma was bright-eyed and saying normal things.

"Oh, Grandma, I'm so lonely," Darcy cried, pressing her head against Grandma's small shoulder.

"You were such a beautiful baby," Grandma said, stroking her hair." 'That one is going to shine like the morning star.' That's what I told your Mama. 'That child is going to shine like the morning star.' Tell me, Angelcake, is your daddy home yet?"

Darcy straightened. "Not yet." Her heart pounded so hard, she could feel it thumping in her chest. Darcy's father had not been home in five years.

"Well, tell him to see me when he gets home. I want him to buy you that blue dress you liked in the store window. That's for you, Angelcake. Tell him I've got money. My social security came, you know. I have money for the blue dress," Grandma said, her eyes slipping shut.

Just then, Darcy heard the apartment door slam. Jamee had come home. Now she stood in the hall, her hands belligerently on her hips. "Are you talking to Grandma again?" Jamee demanded.

"She was talking like normal," Darcy said. "Sometimes she does. You know she does."

"That is so stupid," Jamee snapped. "She never says anything right anymore. Not anything!" Jamee's voice trembled.

Darcy got up quickly and set down the can of malted milk. She ran to Jamee and put her arms around her sister. "Jamee, I know you're hurting too."

"Oh, don't be stupid," Jamee protested, but Darcy hugged her more tightly, and in a few seconds Jamee was crying. "She was the best thing in this stupid house," Jamee cried. "Why'd she have to go?"

"She didn't go," Darcy said. "Not really."

"She did! She did!" Jamee sobbed. She struggled free of Darcy, ran to her room, and slammed the door. In a minute, Darcy heard the bone-rattling sound of rap music.

Want to read more? This and other *Bluford Series™* novels and paperbacks can be purchased for $1 each at www.townsendpress.com.

Teens:
How to Get More Out of This Book

Self-help: The teens who wrote the stories in this book did so because they hope that telling their stories will help readers who are facing similar challenges. They want you to know that you are not alone, and that taking specific steps can help you manage or overcome very difficult situations. They've done their best to be clear about the actions that worked for them so you can see if they'll work for you.

Writing: You can also use the book to improve your writing skills. Each teen in this book wrote 5-10 drafts of his or her story before it was published. If you read the stories closely you'll see that the teens work to include a beginning, a middle, and an end, and good scenes, description, dialogue, and anecdotes (little stories). To improve your writing, take a look at how these writers construct their stories. Try some of their techniques in your own writing.

Reading: Finally, you'll notice that we include the first chapter from a Bluford Series novel in this book, alongside the true stories by teens. We hope you'll like it enough to continue reading. The more you read, the more you'll strengthen your reading skills. Teens at Youth Communication like the Bluford novels because they explore themes similar to those in their own stories. Your school may already have the Bluford books. If not, you can order them online for only $1.

Resources on the Web

We will occasionally post Think About It questions on our website, www.youthcomm.org, to accompany stories in this and other Youth Communication books. We try out the questions with teens and post the ones they like best. Many teens report that writing answers to those questions in a journal is very helpful.

How to Use This Book in Staff Training

Staff say that reading these stories gives them greater insight into what teens are thinking and feeling, and new strategies for working with them. You can help the staff you work with by using these stories as case studies.

Select one story to read in the group, and ask staff to identify and discuss the main issue facing the teen. There may be disagreement about this, based on the background and experience of staff. That is fine. One point of the exercise is that teens have complex lives and needs. Adults can probably be more effective if they don't focus too narrowly and can see several dimensions of their clients.

Ask staff: What issues or feelings does the story provoke in them? What kind of help do they think the teen wants? What interventions are likely to be most promising? Least effective? Why? How would you build trust with the teen writer? How have other adults failed the teen, and how might that affect his or her willingness to accept help? What other resources would be helpful to this teen, such as peer support, a mentor, counseling, family therapy, etc?

Resources on the Web

From time to time we will post Think About It questions on our website, www.youthcomm.org, to accompany stories in this and other Youth Communication books. We try out the questions with teens and post the ones that they find most effective. We'll also post lessons for some of the stories. Adults can use the questions and lessons in workshops.

Discussion Guide

Teachers and Staff:
How to Use This Book in Groups

When working with teens individually or in groups, you can use these stories to help young people face difficult issues in a way that feels safe to them. That's because talking about the issues in the stories usually feels safer to teens than talking about those same issues in their own lives. Addressing issues through the stories allows for some personal distance; they hit close to home, but not too close. Talking about them opens up a safe place for reflection. As teens gain confidence talking about the issues in the stories, they usually become more comfortable talking about those issues in their own lives.

Below are general questions to guide your discussion. In most cases you can read a story and conduct a discussion in one 45-minute session. Teens are usually happy to read the stories aloud, with each teen reading a paragraph or two. (Allow teens to pass if they don't want to read.) It takes 10-15 minutes to read a story straight through. However, it is often more effective to let workshop participants make comments and discuss the story as you go along. The workshop leader may even want to annotate her copy of the story beforehand with key questions.

If teens read the story ahead of time or silently, it's good to break the ice with a few questions that get everyone on the same page: Who is the main character? How old is she? What happened to her? How did she respond? Another good starting question is: "What stood out for you in the story?" Go around the room and let each person briefly mention one thing.

Then move on to open-ended questions, which encourage participants to think more deeply about what the writers were feeling, the choices they faced, and the actions they took. There are no right or wrong answers to the open-ended questions.

Open-ended questions encourage participants to think about how the themes, emotions, and choices in the stories relate to their own lives. Here are some examples of open-ended questions that we have found to be effective. You can use variations of these questions with almost any story in this book.

—What main problem or challenge did the writer face?

—What choices did the teen have in trying to deal with the problem?

—Which way of dealing with the problem was most effective for the teen? Why?

—What strengths, skills, or resources did the teen use to address the challenge?

—If you were in the writer's shoes, what would you have done?

—What could adults have done better to help this young person?

—What have you learned by reading this story that you didn't know before?

—What, if anything, will you do differently after reading this story?

—What surprised you in this story?

—Do you have a different view of this issue, or see a different way of dealing with it, after reading this story? Why or why not?

Credits

The stories in this book originally appeared in the following
Youth Communication publications:

"Opportunity Knocks," by Marcus Fowler, *Represent*, November/December 2003; "A Good Girl's Turmoil," by Ijeoma Okolo, *Represent*, July/August 2001; "She Tells Me She Loves Me," by Cecilia Maneiro, *Represent*, November/December 2003; "Nice While It Lasts," by Anne Ueland, *Represent*, November/December 1999; "The Staff at My Group Home Make a Difference," by Sandra Negron, *Represent*, September/October 1999; "Do the Staff Really Care?" by Anonymous, *Represent*, March/April 1996; "Givin' Props to All Staff and Social Workers," by Jessica DeSince, *Represent*, May/June 1996; "Finding a Father in the System," by Clarissa Venable, *Represent*, January/February 1995; "It May Be Living, But It Ain't Independent!" by Anonymous, *Represent*, May/June 1995; "Here Today, Gone Tomorrow," by Charlene Carter, *Represent*, March/April 2001; "Social Workers: The Good, The Bad, The Overworked," by Shanikqua Crawford, *Represent*, May/June 1999; "Listen Up—Let's Talk!" by Giselle John, *Represent*, March/April 1997; "Looking for Common Ground," by Anzula Richardson, *Represent*, March/April 1994; "Broken Trust," by Anonymous, *Represent*, July/August 2001; "Taming My Anger," by Tray T., *Represent*, November/ December 2007; "Goodbye, Again," by Giselle John, *Represent*, March/April 1997; "A Safe Place," by Donalay Thomas, *Represent*, November/December 2005; "One Tough Mama," by Tashara Gilyard, *Represent*, May/June 2000; "The Worst Part of a Group Home," by Max Moran, *Represent*, July/August 1995; "Me and My Mentor," by Tara Bonaparte, *Represent*, September/October 1998; "A Loner in the Group Home: A New Beginning," by Mohamed Khan, *Represent*, March/April 1995.

About
Youth Communication

Youth Communication, founded in 1980, is a nonprofit youth development program located in New York City whose mission is to teach writing, journalism, and leadership skills. The teenagers we train become writers for our websites and books and for two print magazines: *New Youth Connections*, a general-interest youth magazine, and *Represent*, a magazine by and for young people in foster care.

Each year, up to 100 young people participate in Youth Communication's after school and summer journalism workshops, where they work under the direction of full-time professional editors. Most are African-American, Latino, or Asian, and many are recent immigrants. The opportunity to reach their peers with accurate portrayals of their lives and important self-help information motivates the young writers to create powerful stories.

Our goal is to run a strong youth development program in which teens produce high quality stories that inform and inspire their peers. Doing so requires us to be sensitive to the complicated lives and emotions of the teen participants while also providing an intellectually rigorous experience. We achieve that goal in the writing/teaching/editing relationship, which is the core of our program.

Our teaching and editorial process begins with discussions

between adult editors and the teen staff. In those meetings, the teens and the editors work together to identify the most important issues in the teens' lives and to figure out how those issues can be turned into stories that will resonate with teen readers.

Once story topics are chosen, students begin the process of crafting their stories. For a personal story, that means revisiting events in one's past to understand their significance for the future. For a commentary, it means developing a logical and persuasive point of view. For a reported story, it means gathering information through research and interviews. Students look inward and outward as they try to make sense of their experiences and the world around them and find the points of intersection between personal and social concerns. That process can take a few weeks or a few months. Stories frequently go through 10 or more drafts as students work under the guidance of their editors, the way any professional writer does.

Many of the students who walk through our doors have uneven skills, as a result of poor education, living under extremely stressful conditions, or coming from homes where English is a second language. Yet, to complete their stories, students must successfully perform a wide range of activities, including writing and rewriting, reading, discussion, reflection, research, interviewing, and typing. They must work as members of a team and they must accept individual responsibility. They learn to provide constructive criticism, and to accept it. They engage in explorations of truthfulness, fairness, and accuracy. They meet deadlines. They must develop the audacity to believe that they have something important to say and the humility to recognize that saying it well is not a process of instant gratification. Rather, it usually requires a long, hard struggle through many discussions and much rewriting.

It would be impossible to teach these skills and dispositions as separate, disconnected topics, like grammar, ethics, or assertiveness. However, we find that students make rapid progress when they are learning skills in the context of an inquiry that is personally significant to them and that will benefit their peers.

When teens publish their stories—in *New Youth Connections* and *Represent*, on the Web, and in other publications—they reach tens of thousands of teen and adult readers. Teachers, counselors, social workers, and other adults circulate the stories to young people in their classes and out-of-school youth programs. Adults tell us that teens in their programs—including many who are ordinarily resistant to reading—clamor for the stories. Teen readers report that the stories give them information they can't get anywhere else, and inspire them to reflect on their lives and open lines of communication with adults.

Writers usually participate in our program for one semester, though some stay much longer. Years later, many of them report that working here was a turning point in their lives—that it helped them acquire the confidence and skills that they needed for success in college and careers. Scores of our graduates have overcome tremendous obstacles to become journalists, writers, and novelists. They include National Book Award finalist and MacArthur Fellowship winner Edwidge Danticat, novelist Ernesto Quiñonez, writer Veronica Chambers, and *New York Times* reporter Rachel Swarns. Hundreds more are working in law, business, and other careers. Many are teachers, principals, and youth workers, and several have started nonprofit youth programs themselves and work as mentors—helping another generation of young people develop their skills and find their voices.

Youth Communication is a nonprofit educational corporation. Contributions are gratefully accepted and are tax deductible to the fullest extent of the law.

To make a contribution, or for information about our publications and programs, including our catalog of over 100 books and curricula for hard-to-reach teens, see www.youthcomm.org.

About The Editors

Al Desetta has been an editor of Youth Communication's two teen magazines, *Foster Care Youth United* (now known as *Represent*) and *New Youth Connections*. He was also an instructor in Youth Communication's juvenile prison writing program. In 1991, he became the organization's first director of teacher development, working with high school teachers to help them produce better writers and student publications.

Prior to working at Youth Communication, Desetta directed environmental education projects in New York City public high schools and worked as a reporter.

He has a master's degree in English literature from City College of the City University of New York and a bachelor's degree from the State University of New York at Binghamton, and he was a Revson Fellow at Columbia University for the 1990-91 academic year.

He is the editor of many books, including several other Youth Communication anthologies: *The Heart Knows Something Different: Teenage Voices from the Foster Care System, The Struggle to Be Strong*, and *The Courage to Be Yourself*. He is currently a freelance editor.

Keith Hefner co-founded Youth Communication in 1980 and has directed it ever since. He is the recipient of the Luther P. Jackson Education Award from the New York Association of Black Journalists and a MacArthur Fellowship. He was also a Revson Fellow at Columbia University.

Laura Longhine is the editorial director at Youth Communication. She edited *Represent*, Youth Communication's magazine by and for youth in foster care, for three years, and has written for a variety of publications. She has a BA in English from Tufts University and an MS in Journalism from Columbia University.

More Helpful Books
From Youth Comunication

Do You Have What It Takes? A Comprehensive Guide to Success After Foster Care. In this survival manual, current and former foster teens show how they prepared not only for the practical challenges they've faced on the road to independence, but also the emotional ones. Worksheets and exercises help foster teens plan for their future. Activity pages at the end of each chapter help social workers, independent living instructors, and other leaders use the stories with individuals or in groups. (Youth Communication)

The Struggle to Be Strong: True Stories by Teens About Overcoming Tough Times. Foreword by Veronica Chambers. Help young people identify and build on their own strengths with 30 personal stories about resiliency. (Free Spirit)

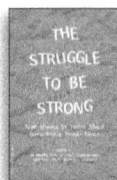

Depression, Anger, Sadness: Teens Write About Facing Difficult Emotions. Give teens the confidence they need to seek help when they need it. These teens write candidly about difficult emotional problems—such as depression, cutting, and domestic violence—and how they have tried to help themselves. (Youth Communication)

Out of the Shadows: Teens Write About Surviving Sexual Abuse. Help teens feel less alone and more hopeful about overcoming the trauma of sexual abuse. This collection includes first-person accounts by male and female survivors grappling with fear, shame, and guilt. (Youth Communication)

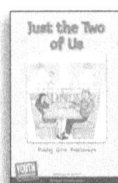

Just the Two of Us: Teens Write About Building Good Relationships. Show teens how to make and maintain healthy relationships (and avoid bad ones). Many teens in care have had poor role models and are emotionally vulnerable. These stories demonstrate good and bad choices teens make in friendship and romance. (Youth Communication)

The Fury Inside: Teens Write About Anger. Help teens manage their anger. These writers show how they got better control of their emotions and sought the support of others. (Youth Communication)

Always on the Move: Teens Write About Changing Homes and Staff. Help teens feel less alone with these stories about how their peers have coped with the painful experience of frequent placement changes, and turnover among staff and social workers. (Youth Communication)

Two Moms in My Heart: Teens Write About the Adoption Option. Teens will appreciate these stories by peers who describe how complicated the adoption experience can be—even when it should give them a more stable home than foster care. (Youth Communication)

My Secret Addiction: Teens Write About Cutting. These true accounts of cutting, or self-mutilation, offer a window into the personal and family situations that lead to this secret habit, and show how teens can get the help they need. (Youth Communication)

Growing Up Together: Teens Write About Being Parents. Give teens a realistic view of the conflicts and burdens of parenthood with these stories from real teen parents. The stories also reveal how teens grew as individuals by struggling to become responsible parents. (Youth Communication)

To order these and other books, go to:
www.youthcomm.org
or call 212-279-0708 x115

www.ingramcontent.com/pod-product-compliance
Lightning Source LLC
Chambersburg PA
CBHW051742090426
42738CB00010B/2371